KEYNOTE MASTERY

THE PERSONAL JOURNEY OF A
PROFESSIONAL SPEAKER

PATRICK SCHWERDTFEGER

AUTHORITY
PUBLISHING

Keynote Mastery: The Personal Journey of a Professional Speaker
By Patrick Schwerdtfeger

BIO026000 BIOGRAPHY & AUTOBIOGRAPHY / Personal Memoirs
BIO003000 BIOGRAPHY & AUTOBIOGRAPHY / Business
BUS046000 BUSINESS & ECONOMICS / Motivational

ISBN-10: 1-935953-70-2
ISBN-13: 978-1-935953-70-8

Cover design by Lewis Agrell
Interior design by JETLAUNCH

Printed in the United States of America

Authority Publishing
11230 Gold Express Dr. #310-413
Gold River, CA 95670
800-877-1097
www.AuthorityPublishing.com

CONTENTS

FOREWORD

BY DAN NAINAN

I first came to know about Patrick Schwerdtfeger in quite an unusual fashion. I'm a comedian and speaker, and received an invitation from an archbishop in South Africa to speak at an event in Cape Town. This was nothing unusual, as I routinely get invitations to speak all over the world. In fact, I performed in Durban, South Africa a few years ago and had a wonderful experience there. As I emailed back and forth with this archbishop, however, I became a bit suspicious about whether this was really a legitimate offer.

As a friend suggested to me, I input the name of the church and the word "scam" into Google. I was shocked to find that another speaker had been contacted with a very similar-sounding offer several years previous, and that he had been ripped off. Apparently, this scenario is quite common. In essence, the scam consists of offering the speaker a fee of $10,000 or more, and then when the speaker accepts, the archbishop's secretary insists that the speaker send a couple of thousand dollars ahead of time for visa fees. Patrick had been approached by the same people and published a blog post about the experience, warning other speakers about the scam. I was very fortunate to find his post and as a result, did not fall victim to the ruse.

I wrote to Patrick and thanked him profusely for the blog post and for helping his fellow speakers. Patrick was very gregarious and wrote back quickly. We struck up a relationship via email and have stayed in touch ever since.

As I learned more about Patrick, I was truly fascinated by his story. Many speakers become speakers because they went through a traumatic experience, or they had something extraordinary happen to them, like landing an airplane in a river, or winning the Olympics, or cutting off an arm to save their life, and so forth. Patrick had no such background, and yet, he's managed to become a highly sought after speaker who travels all over the world.

I recently had the distinct privilege of meeting Patrick in person. I was booked to perform in the San Francisco Bay Area and emailed him to see if he wanted to get together for coffee. Despite his busy schedule, he accepted, and we met near his home. After a few minutes of having coffee, Patrick generously invited me to come to his home for a nutritious and spicy bowl of homemade chicken curry. I'm constantly hungry, and this meal hit the spot. I came away from our meeting feeling motivated, inspired (and quite full).

For me, Patrick's book has been an amazingly accurate reflection of my own career. There were so many stories that mirrored my own experiences. The crazy situations that have dotted my own journey aren't that unusual after all! Anyone who is already in the process of building a public career will find familiar circumstances on every page. And for those just getting started, this is an invaluable guide to the adventures ahead.

Becoming a successful speaker isn't as much about innate talent as it is about repetition, hard work and dogged determination, as well as an undying belief in oneself and a desire to make the world a better place. Patrick is a shining example of such a person.

Some studies suggest that fewer than 10 percent of people truly enjoy their jobs, and many dream of breaking free and finding their true passion. They want to do what they were truly meant to do. These dreams are definitely possible, but it's a lot easier if you know what to expect. Whatever your profession and whatever you'd like to become one day, this book provides a roadmap for the path forward. It will help you realize your dream.

I know you'll love this book as much as I did. Enjoy!

ACKNOWLEDGEMENTS

This is the most personal book I have ever written and I am grateful to those who read early versions and provided candid—and sometimes harsh—feedback. The finished product is better because of their comments and suggestions.

Maria Picciani in Melbourne, Australia, was the first person to read it. Thank you, Maria! Your comments started the process and led indirectly to hundreds of changes. I can't wait for you to read this final version. It's quite different from the original manuscript.

My sister, Annette, made an enormous commitment to read and edit my work as well. Annette, I was stunned by your attention to detail and am delighted that you took the time to read about my dreams and adventures.

Michael Larsen was the literary agent for my third book, "Marketing Shortcuts for the Self-Employed," and was kind enough to read through my manuscript and provide edits and direction. Michael, I am grateful for your guidance and generosity.

Stephanie Chandler is the owner of Authority Publishing, the company that published this title. She also read my manuscript and provided valuable advice throughout this process. Many thanks, Stephanie, for your experience and your acumen.

Richard Bolles helped me completely rewrite the first chapter. Before he restructured it, it was a mess. Richard, thank you for taking time away from your vacation in Carmel to provide such valuable feedback.

Dan Nainan, I'm thrilled that you found me online last year. We certainly have lots in common and I have enormous respect for your work. Thank you for agreeing to write the foreword for this book. And thanks as well for pointing out all the dangling participles in the early versions.

Bryan Beyer, Wendy Rosenthal, Manu Kalia and Omaid Homayun also provided valuable suggestions. Bryan, thank you for your detailed email synopsis. Wendy, thank you for thinking about my target audience and helping me refine my message. Manu, thank you for helping me keep the 20%. And Omaid, thank you for helping me trim the fat.

I invited the members of my Entrepreneur & Small Business Academy to edit the manuscript as well and 37 people volunteered. The first person to return feedback was Elaine Starling, and her comments were among the most detailed I received. Jimmy Dang was also extremely specific with his suggestions. Thank you both.

The group also included Michelle Kingman, Fred Fuld, Beth Barany, Christopher Niem Henley, Karl Palachuck, Evelyn Rolley, Neema Saini, John Chang and David Mitroff. Thank you for taking the time to read my work and provide feedback.

I felt compelled to write this book and am grateful for all the support I received during the process. Many thanks to all who contributed.

PREFACE

What's required to achieve success? What's the secret to fame and fortune? There are countless gurus offering tips and tricks, but the truth is that success requires that you walk the path, one foot in front of the other, pushing forward regardless of the obstacles until people start recognizing and appreciating the journey you've traveled. The journey *becomes* the destination.

Over the past seven years, I have earned over 90% of my income in speaking fees. It's an unconventional career and people ask me about it all the time. They ask me how I got here. They ask me how it happened. I love answering those questions because I'm proud of what I've accomplished. There were so many obstacles along the way. There were so many challenges. But after years of pursuing my dream, I have now constructed a respectable career as a professional keynote speaker.

This book is the long version of my answers to those questions. It includes the whole story. It's raw and personal, but that's the nature of stories like this one. Success doesn't emerge from a vacuum. It emerges when a human being dedicates their life to an ambitious goal, and it usually involves plenty of personal struggles along the way. Those struggles are important because they build the depth of character needed to embrace success when it finally arrives.

I sincerely hope you find value in this book. While it definitely includes a lot of how-to advice for aspiring speakers (and for self-employed professionals in general), it is also a memoir. The majority of chapters recount stories from my journey. They narrate the evolution of my career. By the end, you will know more about me than most of my friends do.

Many of the stories probably resemble experiences you've had as well; at least I hope they do. The journey to success is innately human. We are not robots. We are people with hopes and fears and victories and setbacks. Success depends on how we respond to the changing circumstances of our lives. I didn't always respond well, but thankfully, I managed to maintain a forward trajectory.

I am quite eager to hear from my readers. There are a number of ways to continue the dialog and I have referenced them throughout the book. In the meantime, I invite you into my life. Enjoy the journey. I can't wait to hear your thoughts on the other side.

ON TOP OF THE WORLD

There were only two buttons in the elevator: "C" for Concourse (the ground level) and "123" for the 123rd floor. The Burj Khalifa is the tallest skyscraper on the planet (as tall as the CN Tower in Toronto with the Eiffel Tower in Paris stacked on top of it), and the architects included a 123-story elevator shaft reserved exclusively for the patrons of Atmosphere, the world's highest restaurant.

It feels like the *Guinness Book of World Records* was written here. The world's largest shopping mall is attached to the world's tallest building, which boasts the world's highest restaurant, the world's highest swimming pool and the world's most expensive condominium. The elevator I was standing in is the world's fastest and longest.

It took less than one minute for the elevator to reach its destination 442 meters above the lobby but for me, the trip seemed to last forever. I was reflecting about the previous six days. The 18th Annual GCC eGovernment and eServices Conference had gone well. It was my first trip to Dubai and the 350 delegates who attended the conference were very different from my normal audience.

I had dreamt about speaking in Dubai since 2008 and here I was, looking back on it after the fact. My dream had actually come true and it hadn't gone unnoticed by my Facebook friends who had spent the week commenting on the photos and videos I was posting. It seemed like my speaking career was finally turning the corner.

Two hours earlier, I was on stage, answering a few final questions for these perfectly dressed Arabs. Arab men wear white robes here in Dubai and the women wear black. Most of the men wear white headscarves but those from Saudi Arabia use red-and-white checkered cloth instead. The men from Oman wear headdresses that wrap around their heads similar to the Sikhs I had met while speaking in India two years earlier. These white robes are called *Thawbs* and Arab men take as much pride in them as I do in my suits. They're always perfectly pressed and immaculately clean. The robes reflect their status, and few things are more important than status in the opulent luxury of Dubai.

To me, they all looked very similar, like uniformed delegates in a science-fiction film. But to them, we westerners all look similar as well, wearing our suits and ties. And even though I was proud of the custom-tailored suits I wore during the five-day conference, the Arabs probably couldn't distinguish them from the standard Men's Wearhouse brands.

My first session was on the first day of the conference. The topic was a significant departure for the government officials and IT professionals that dominated the audience. Most of the sessions were technical case histories about eGovernment initiatives around the Middle East region. Mine was about global megatrends and how they would affect these initiatives in the future. So most of the sessions were specific and precise but mine was broad and general.

The session went reasonably well. I got through my slides. I delivered my presentation but never felt like the audience engaged with my message. During lunch that day, two men offered compliments and one a critique. Despite the mixed reviews, my books were selling well and that remains the ultimate measure of success for a professional speaker.

People reveal their true opinions with their pocketbooks. If a session goes well and the audience engages with the talk, book sales are brisk. But if the talk falls flat, nobody buys. Financially, it really doesn't matter. I only earn 91¢ for each book. You don't earn much on book sales, but it reflects the audience engagement and that's important.

There was an awards ceremony on Monday evening and my second speaking opportunity took place there. The ceremony was the highlight of the conference and was held in the Burj Al Arab seven-star hotel. It's an iconic building shaped like a huge sail that sits on its own man-made island. At night, they project a colorful lightshow onto the 60-story translucent white canvas that makes up its west wall.

The ceremony was attended by three members of the royal family and a number of government ministers. There were three white Rolls Royce Phantoms parked by the front lobby. The ballroom, located immediately below the helicopter pad, was besieged by paparazzi-style video crews and photographers. We had to wait an hour and twenty minutes for the award-winners to descend from their VIP lounge and I was instructed to address the audience as "Your excellences, distinguished guests, ladies and gentlemen."

I pinched myself hundreds of times during these six days. How is it possible that a guy like me ends up in Dubai, speaking in front of 350 government officials from oil-rich nations in the Middle East? My father passed away three years earlier but I still speak to him regularly in prayer. I spoke to him many times that week and sensed he was equally amazed by the adventure that I found myself on.

My third speaking session was the most successful of the three. I could tell that the audience was embracing my content because I could see nodding headscarves scattered throughout the conference room. It always amazes me how the human eye can pick up a one-inch nod in an audience of hundreds. When I'm on stage, I notice nods immediately and use them as a barometer of engagement. My books sold out by lunchtime.

I was invited on stage one last time on Wednesday morning along with three other western speakers wearing suits and ties, to answer any remaining questions. My speaking obligations were now finished.

I had promised myself this elevator ride, this ride to the Atmosphere restaurant in the Burj Khalifa, as my reward for finishing successfully. The elevator doors opened on the 123rd floor, and Boyd and I walked out. Boyd was one of the other western speakers. He was from Amsterdam and spoke in the mind-numbing vernacular of management consultants and corporate contractors. His PowerPoint slides were a collection of "knowledge maps" and "intelligence architectures." It was both inspiring and intimidating to attend his sessions. But he was also extraordinarily kind and was my primary companion while in Dubai. He had been here many times before and showed me around.

We were greeted as we stepped into the restaurant lobby and escorted to our table up one more flight of stairs to the 124th floor. We were just there for tea but it cost about $85 each. Oh well, this was the tallest restaurant in the world. They could charge whatever they wanted. I certainly wasn't going to miss this opportunity and neither were countless others who paid the same amount to see what Dubai looked like from above.

Unfortunately, the view was awful. The air had become thicker every day since my arrival. The culprit: sand. The desert sand in Dubai is incredibly fine and when the wind picks up, the sky fills with a thick yellowy haze. Even on a calm day, your eyes burn. I noticed it the day I arrived and my eyes never adjusted. This was the worst day so far and we could hardly see the 70- and 80-story condominium towers that seemed so small from our perch above.

Even still, the unique top-down perspective didn't go unnoticed. 70- and 80-story towers are impressive in any other context but from the 124th floor, they seem small. Here I was, on top of the world, and the only reason I was there was because I had the audacity to send my marketing materials to international destinations, when most speakers focused on local markets.

Four years earlier, I learned that the hardest place to get paid to speak is in your own backyard. I had submitted a proposal to speak in Sweden and it was accepted. Why? Because I was an American from Silicon Valley—I was from far away. That's what made me interesting. Jesus once said that no man is a prophet in his own land. I went to Sweden and was welcomed with open arms, and it led me to market my services in the most exotic global destinations I could find.

This trip to Dubai was a perfect example. I send marketing packages to event planners all around the world and that effort eventually led to this improbable trip. I was now standing in the world's tallest restaurant, looking down at the surrounding skyscrapers. Norman Vincent Peale once said, "Shoot for the moon. Even if you miss, you'll land among the stars." That's exactly what this week felt like.

THIS BOOK'S PURPOSE

This book recounts my journey as a professional speaker, told in 65 short chapters describing some of the most improbable stories you can imagine. It includes countless lessons and insights that I've learned, as well as 16 worksheets to help you apply these lessons in your own career. If you would like to become a professional speaker, this is a great resource. It will give you a detailed description of the process and the situations you may encounter along the way.

As I mentioned, this is not exclusively a how-to book. It's also a memoir. It's my story and it's very different from the story of most professional speakers. It's a story of loneliness, but it's also a story of victory. It's a story of brute force and the power of determination. It's a story of incremental successes and step-by-step progress, and it will be the most honest and transparent account you will ever find on this topic.

Most speakers accomplish something incredible in some other field and only then become speakers. They go on to spend the rest of their lives speaking about that one accomplishment. I'm not like that. I started with no real credential and built my career from the ground up. That's what makes it so remarkable. I didn't have the traditional prerequisites and I made it anyway. That means anyone can do this. It's a process of incremental victories and it can be replicated.

People who have these incredible accomplishments don't need any help becoming successful. If you're the guy who won gold at the Olympics, you don't need any help becoming famous. You're already there. If you're the quarterback of the Dallas Cowboys, you don't need any help. If you're the #1 stock trader on Wall Street or the world chess champion, you don't need any help. By definition, these people are few and far between and people instinctively want to hear their stories.

On January 15, 2009, Captain "Sully" Sullenberger landed US Airways flight #1549 in the Hudson River in New York City after the plane flew through a flock of Canadian geese. All 155 passengers and crewmembers survived. This is a perfect example: Captain "Sully" Sullenberger did something truly remarkable and became a well-deserved hero as a result. After that event, he immediately became a highly paid speaker.

In 2003, Aron Lee Ralston cut off his own right forearm with a dull pocketknife after getting stuck under a dislodged boulder while hiking in Utah. That's insane! Nobody's debating that. He did something truly incredible and promptly became a professional speaker afterwards. Their speaking careers are perfectly reasonable and thoroughly deserved, but they're not common.

I never did anything that incredible. I think I'm a smart guy and I'm definitely very stubborn and determined, but I never had a huge victory in my life. I built my career one step at a time, slowly building my credibility and improving my marketing and learning the ins and outs of the business. Now, I have become successful in my career. I earn over 90% of my income from speaking fees and have spoken professionally in dozens of cities around the world.

This book is about achieving success when you're starting out as an average person. There are no caveats to these strategies. There are no prerequisites. If you want to become a professional speaker, I know how to do it because I've done it myself. With enough determination and tenacity, anyone can do the same thing—and I guarantee this book will accelerate your progress.

Download the worksheets at the KeynoteMastery.com website. There are many lessons and industry secrets in this book, and I have distilled them down into actionable checklists that are included in these downloadable PDF files. You will also have an opportunity to join the Keynote Mastery community, which I'll tell you more about later.

This book is a perfect guide for just about any self-employed professional. Are you a real estate agent or insurance broker? Or perhaps you're a financial planner or a chiropractor. Maybe you're a life coach or a business consultant or a physical therapist or a dentist. In any of these fields, the marketing objective is to build credibility and exposure, positioning yourself as an authority in your field. This book is explicitly about that process.

Speaking is a great way to develop your reputation and become a recognized expert in your field, but that's not the only thing I'm advocating. I'm encouraging you to think bigger about your business and the role you play in your industry. The stories in this book and the chronology of the process serve as a detailed roadmap for people striving to build their own identities, and I sincerely hope they provide that value for you.

At the same time, this book is a memoir. It's my story. There were so many crazy things that happened along the way, I just *had* to write them down. The journey was full of irony and serendipitous happenings. It was full of struggle and frustration but it was also full of victories and self-discovery. It has given me tremendous joy to recount all those memories in this work.

The chapters are ordered chronologically but the time frames often overlap because each sequence of events evolved from previous circumstances, and then impacted future adventures as well. We live a linear existence but there are always different storylines playing out simultaneously in our lives. That was certainly true on my journey and is reflected in this book.

My friends frequently call me out on my direct communication style. I naturally gravitate to the cold, harsh truth and try to confront stark realities before getting too excited about future possibilities. You'll find that style throughout this book. The reality is that self-employment is the hardest thing I've ever done but it's also the most rewarding—by far. I will describe the challenges as well as the victories.

There was no shortage of financial and emotional trauma along the way and that is probably best represented by my rising and falling credit card balances. I once compiled a chart of my monthly balances over a seven-year period and it tells an amazingly detailed story of my journey. Not surprisingly, the emotional swings follow the financial ones. To help you appreciate the context behind all the experiences in this book, I've included periodic references to my credit card balances where appropriate.

For some, my level of indebtedness may seem insignificant. I know there are people who take on huge debts to pursue their dreams and I have plenty of respect for those people. Also, people who own homes are used to seeing large loan balances on their monthly statements and may, as a result, also feel like my emotional struggles with debt were unjustified. But for me, they were the largest debts I ever had and for a long time, I just didn't see how I would pay them all back.

The net result is the most transparent piece of work I have ever published. You will get to know me quite well in the pages ahead. You'll see the good, the bad and the ugly. But you will also see the eventual victory and how it materialized, slowly but surely, over a seven-year period. It was an incredible journey and I can't wait to tell you about it, so let's get started.

3

LISTENING

I've wanted to become a speaker ever since I was 10 or 12 years old. I don't remember the exact age but I used to watch people speaking in front of audiences and be overcome with envy. I wanted to be up there myself. I wanted to be the one delivering the message.

It would happen every Sunday at church. We had two very good priests. They had near-opposite styles but both had a gift for delivering good sermons. Every week as the Gospel was being read, I would start wondering what the priest would say next during his sermon. What would his message be this week?

There was always a pause between the end of the Gospel reading and the beginning of the sermon. The priest would close the Bible, take a breath and then begin his sermon. I would tingle with anticipation during that pause. I couldn't wait for the sermon to begin.

The older of the two priests was Father Mugford. He was much more conservative and deliberate, but his sermons were well thought out and always had an interesting angle. He was an intellectual. He was smart. Many times, he would incorporate recent news stories, either local or on the other side of the world, and anchor his message—his lessons learned—to that situation.

My mother was always well read. She read the newspaper on the living-room couch each evening and always knew the latest happenings around the world. She loved to talk about those things, so the four of us kids had a regular dose of the news at home. Father Mugford's sermons added dimension to those news stories. They added perspective.

The younger of the two priests was Father Landry. He was awesome. He was an overweight guy but it suited him really well. He had a beard and had a very casual style. He was funny and could find almost any reason to start laughing. My brother and I were altar boys growing up and we always loved it when Father Landry was doing the Mass.

Father Landry had a very different style than Father Mugford, but they complemented each other. Father Landry's sermons were often funny and very practical. He was casual. It didn't seem like he was a priest at all. It was like he was a camp counselor. But yet again, he always found ways to incorporate interesting perspectives in his sermons. I loved it.

These priests weren't the only speakers I idolized as a child. I grew up in Canada and loved watching Brian Mulroney speak. He was the Prime Minister of Canada at that time—first elected in 1984 when I was 13 years old—and had a very strong speaking style. He was often dramatic, once tearing apart a piece of legislation during his speech and throwing the papers on the floor. Anything could happen when Brian Mulroney was speaking. You never knew what to expect, but he had passion and I was enthralled.

Of course, Ronald Reagan was elected in the United States in 1980 and had an amazing style of his own. Like Father Landry, he was a bit more casual and often told these canned, somewhat tacky jokes, but he was good at it. He delivered those jokes so well, and everyone came to expect them from him. Audiences listened with anticipation as he told his jokes, waiting eagerly for the punch line. Meanwhile, he also had an incredible ability to weave poignant messages into his speeches. By the end, you always felt inspired but also entertained.

Similar to Franklin Delano Roosevelt, Ronald Reagan was famous for his fireside chats, a speaking style that I identified with strongly. Years later, as a professional speaker, I would try to create that intimate dynamic with my own audiences. More on that later.

My fascination with speakers had a distinct quality for many years. At that time, I believed that I knew what they were going to say ahead of time. As they were saying any given sentence, I would automatically guess at the upcoming words and phrases and try to speak along with them in unison.

All of these speakers were different from each other, but each one's style had its own rhythm, its own cadence. I would pick up on it immediately and try to finish their sentences for them. Many times, I was right. When you're in tune with a particular speaking style, it's amazing how accurately you can predict upcoming phrases before they're actually spoken.

For many years when I was young, I thought it as a special ability. I thought it was my own secret superpower. It seemed so natural. I would correctly finish their sentences so often that I thought I was literally reading their minds. I know now that it's not uncommon for people to notice these types of speaking rhythms, but I did pick up on them early in life and used them to anticipate what they would say next.

Of course, I wasn't *always* right. And when I was wrong, my mind would automatically decide which version I liked better: theirs or mine. In that sense, I was definitely an egotistical kid. I almost always liked my version better! Every time I listened to a speaker, I would inevitably find areas where I thought they could've expressed something better. I instinctively thought of ways the speech could've been more effective.

I don't remember specific examples from my younger years but a great example happened when Barack Obama spoke at the memorial service after a mass shooting in Arizona that targeted US Congresswoman Gabrielle Giffords in 2011. Whether you like Obama or hate him, he has a gift for delivering speeches and was definitely effective in conveying the emotions of that event—but in my opinion, he also missed an opportunity to deepen the connection with the audience.

Obama was speaking about Christina-Taylor Green, the nine-year old girl who was killed in the shooting. He spoke about her with eloquence and compassion but when his references to her were finished, he moved right along to a section of hope and gratitude for the people who survived the shooting, including Gabrielle Giffords herself. I was stunned that he left out a reference to his own daughters.

The memorial service took place on January 12, 2011. Obama's two daughters, Sasha and Malia, were nine and 13 at that time. It would've been extraordinarily touching for him to say "Christina was just nine years old" and then pause and perhaps glance up and to the left briefly, and then continue "My youngest is nine too." That one sentence would've brought his role as a father into the speech. It would've demonstrated the personal nature of his grief.

These are tiny details but they make a huge difference. My mind has always focused on these things, trying to find better and more effective ways of communicating ideas. Obama is an amazing speaker, as is Ronald Reagan, Brian Mulroney and the two priests from my neighborhood church. And each one of them has impressed me countless times with their eloquence and style, but they have also each had opportunities to say things even better.

When you listen to a speaker, ask yourself how you would communicate the same message. Would you word it differently? What would've made the speech more impactful for you? Strive to cultivate awareness. Strive to become more aware. That awareness will help you build your career.

NATURE VERSUS NURTURE

My problem growing up was that I never felt justified to express my opinion, not only with respect to speeches I had watched but with just about everything else as well. I was never the smart one in my family. I always valued "street smarts" over "book smarts," but the rest of my family felt differently. Academically, they all had me beat.

My father was a professor of solid-state physics at the University of British Columbia (UBC) in Vancouver. He had a PhD and was definitely a smart cookie. Both of my sisters got PhDs in organic chemistry. The oldest one married a PhD in robotics and the other one married a PhD in biological sciences. They all work in ivory-tower institutions.

My brother was brilliant as well but less scientific than my sisters. He used to read the *National Geographic* from cover to cover, and remember every word. When I had school projects, I used to ask my brother to tell me about the War of 1812, for example, and he would describe the circumstances behind the conflict as if he had lived through them himself. He was a walking encyclopedia.

Anyway, they all seemed so much smarter than me. They got good grades at school. They were never particularly social and didn't have tons of friends, but they won awards and got academic scholarships. I was the opposite. I wanted to socialize and have friends. I wanted jobs in the real world. I wanted to meet different types of people and hear their stories. I wanted to have personal conversations with perfect strangers and see if I could get them to tell me their inner most secrets. It was sport for me and school just didn't compare.

I did okay in most of my classes but usually got B's and C's, not the A's that my siblings brought home. My parents valued school. My mother, in particular, was focused on report cards. She grew up in Switzerland and had only one measure of a person's worth: being cultured and refined. I got to know those two words well growing up. It was the only thing that mattered to her. And believe me: there was nothing cultured or refined about the jobs I was getting or the socializing I was doing.

The point is that I felt quite inferior as a child, not in a worldly sense but in an academic sense. As a result, I was always uncomfortable when voicing my opinion. It was frustrating for me because I almost always had something that I wanted to say. I always had an opinion, but I just didn't feel confident spitting it out. In fact, if I had an opinion on something, I would say that I read it in some publication like a magazine or the newspaper. That way, I was just the messenger and nobody could criticize my stupid idea. It wasn't mine. It was someone else's.

When babies learn to speak, they almost always say "mama" or "dada" first. Makes sense, but that's not what happened with me. The first words I ever spoke were "ich weiss es," which is German for "I know it." Sad but true. I always thought I knew everything. It didn't really matter what my mother or father said, I replied with "ich weiss es." Stop talking! I know that already!!

Am I a narcissist? I don't know. Maybe. Believe me; I have plenty of insecurities. I've never been brashly egotistical, but I always had this strong inner belief that I knew things and that my opinions needed to be heard. I've been that way since I was literally one year old. I guess I found the perfect career. I get paid to share my opinions!

This is a nature-versus-nurture discussion. I had both. My father was a teacher and so are my sisters, and they're all good at it. My oldest sister, Annette, once took a physics course that my father was teaching and she used to tell us how kind and patient he was in that role. He never said that much at home but in his classroom, he guided his students through complicated subjects and excelled at explaining complicated concepts.

My mother was a teacher as well. For years, she gave piano lessons in our home but she also gave tours at the Museum of Anthropology (MOA) on the UBC campus. The museum featured Pacific Northwest Coast Native Indian art like totem poles and elaborate masks. She was known to give the best tour of all the volunteers. She knew her subject and explained it with clarity and passion.

So I definitely have the nurture element. I grew up in a family of teachers and, essentially, became one myself. They didn't necessarily tell me how to be a good teacher but they were good teachers themselves and I learned many of the skills by osmosis. But I also had the nature element. I was born this way. I've always had something to say and was always passionate about expressing it effectively.

EARLY SUCCESSES

This combination of nature and nurture followed me through my entire life. I had a number of occasions where I ended up being the spokesperson within my peer group. I created a new game called "Spinner" in 6th grade and presented it to my local school board. I represented student interests on the Vancouver Safety Council from 1987 to 1989. I was selected to travel to Ottawa for the Rotary Club's "Adventures in Citizenship" program in 1988.

That trip convinced me to later study business at Carleton University in Ottawa. During my second and third year, I started a little business giving exam-prep courses in Micro and Macro Economics. In my third year, I ran (but didn't win) for the student government in the on-campus residence complex. In my fourth year, I competed in the Canadian Business Competitions on the debating team. It seemed like one way or another, I was constantly finding opportunities to speak publicly.

The trend continued after I graduated. One of my first "career" jobs was with Pimlico Apparel in Vancouver. They had a division that sold denim shirts and jackets to the promotional products industry. I was hired as their Credit Manager but was soon asked to help set up their sales department (which hadn't existed previously). I split up the United States into four territories and selected the West Coast territory as my own. The job involved attending trade shows and setting up sales appointments with distributors throughout the 13 western states.

The head of merchandizing for the company was a guy named Roy Rolston. He was an older guy who had a stylish beard and always wore trendy clothes, and he was extremely passionate about our product line. We were a premium producer. We used the same high-quality denim that Guess and The Gap used, along with superior felled seams in the garment construction. These quality distinctions were fascinating to me and I incorporated those little details into my sales presentations.

The distributors loved those little details. It made them look smart in front of their own corporate customers. Later, I worked for two other suppliers and again incorporated production details into my presentations. My goal was to reveal the hidden secrets behind those products, secrets they would never notice in a catalog. Most people didn't know those details and the salespeople who attended my presentations loved learning about them. It made them feel like insiders.

This became the hallmark of my speaking style. I wanted my audiences to feel like they received something special. They got a secret that most people didn't have. Years later, I would refer to this as the "surprising truth." I wanted to challenge a conventionally held belief and reveal an alternative way of looking at the situation. It didn't matter what the topic was, I just needed to find that surprising truth and then the rest of my presentation would come together naturally.

It was during these years in sales that I began to embrace speaking as my true calling. It was the one thing that always went well for me. I was good at it. The problem was that professional speakers always seemed to have accomplished something incredible in their pasts; some undeniable victory that they could then leverage as a speaker. It would be many years before I realized that an indisputable victory wasn't actually required at all.

People naturally gravitate to the things they're good at. What do *you* gravitate to? Have you regularly found yourself speaking in front of people? Do you instinctively seek leadership, teaching or sales capacities? If so, it might be time to embrace that skillset as your calling. Trust me; it's a gift and can lead to an amazing career.

THE LAND OF OPPORTUNITY

O ne of the most exciting phone calls I ever received was from my own sister in March, 1998. She told me that I qualified to get a US passport. I was stunned. I was born in Vancouver, Canada, but my father grew up in Philadelphia and then moved to Vancouver in his late twenties. We asked him if we qualified for US citizenship when we were growing up, but he didn't know much about it and dismissed it as unlikely. He didn't seem to understand why we even cared about such a silly idea.

Meanwhile, the American economy was more than 10 times the size of the Canadian economy. It's the land of opportunity. Most of the shows on TV featured American experiences in American cities and for a business-oriented kid like me, the allure was impossible to ignore. California, in particular, seemed like a business utopia. If you wanted to go big in life, California was the place to be!

After getting her PhD, my sister moved down to Indiana on an H1B Visa and her employer subsequently initiated a green-card application without her knowledge. That's not allowed. H1B Visas are temporary by definition and green cards are permanent. You're not allowed to do both at the same time. Also, the H1B requires that the person go back to his or her home country once each year to renew. Meanwhile, when you're applying for a green card, you're not allowed to leave the country. So right there, the two conflict directly with each other.

Without knowing about the active green-card application, she came back to Canada in 1998 to renew her H1B Visa and was then turned away when she tried to re-enter the United States. She and her husband were stranded in a Canadian border town for a week while they tried to get it sorted out. Once the Immigration Services reviewed her file and saw that she was born to an American father, they let her back in. She called me that day and my life immediately took a hard left-hand turn.

The process was a bit more complicated for me than it was for her. My parents had registered the birth of their first three children with the US State Department but for whatever reason, they never did it for me. That meant I had to submit a ton of paperwork to prove that my dad lived in America as an American citizen for at least ten years prior to my birth, at least five of which were after his 14th birthday.

These seemly arbitrary requirements were the result of a law passed shortly after the Korean War. During that conflict, there were a number of children born to American fathers and Korean mothers. Those children were ostracized in Korea and because they were born outside America, they didn't qualify for US citizenship either. So in response to that set of circumstances, Congress passed a law (7 FAM 1133.2-2 Immigration and Nationality Act (INA) of 1952, Section 301) allowing foreign-born babies to qualify for citizenship as long as the American parent had lived in America for at least 10 years before the child was born. That bizarre piece of legislation allowed me to qualify.

It took months for me to accumulate the documentation I needed. I got transcripts from my dad's schools and medical records from his healthcare providers. It was a big pile of red tape and it cost a bundle in processing fees but once complete, I submitted the file to the American embassy and got my passport two weeks later. And because I had already been traveling in my West Coast territory and knew many of the suppliers in the industry, I lined up a job while I was waiting for the processing and moved to Los Angeles just six days after getting my passport.

It was a crazy time for me. I didn't even have a social security number! Getting an apartment was a challenge because they couldn't pull my credit report. I had no American credit cards either but I tackled those challenges one after the other and ended up getting settled fairly quickly. I was 27 years old and living in LA! It was a whole new world for me: endless concrete freeways, palm trees and sandy beaches ... I was in paradise.

Less than two years later, with the dotcom bubble inflating quickly, I was offered a job at an online promotional products distributor in the San Francisco Bay Area. I loved LA and still do but at that time, the Internet revolution seemed unstoppable and I moved up to Oakland on January 30th, 2000, and started my new job on February 1st. Unfortunately, the stock market crashed during the following month and the layoffs started shortly thereafter.

I was pretty good at building alliances and survived the first twelve rounds of layoffs. My salary was reduced twice during that time but I never lost my job. After the twelfth round, the CEO took me aside and told me that he didn't know where to put me after the thirteenth round. I laughed. "Put me on the list!" It was awful being part of a failing venture and I was ready to try something new. I was laid off on September 29th, 2002, and have been self-employed ever since.

THE STRUGGLE BEGINS

S elf-employment was difficult. I tried a variety of things over those first three years but nothing hit the mark. My ventures included business brokerage financing, mobile notary work and, finally, real estate mortgages. I either enjoyed the work but made no money, or I made good money but hated the work. I had yet to embrace the professional speaking business and was struggling to pay my bills.

I always had a simple way to measure my own success: I wanted "a lifestyle commensurate with my skillset." My skillset was good. If I were in corporate America, I'm sure I would've been making good money, but that's not the path I chose and I had absolutely no idea how to jumpstart my career.

It boils down to shame. I was ashamed of my situation. My lifestyle was pathetic, yet I had a good skillset to work with. It didn't make sense. People who knew me wondered why I had yet to succeed. Behind my back, I'm sure they wondered what was secretly wrong with me. I hated that disparity between my theoretical worth (based on my skills and personality) and my actual worth in reality. I absolutely did *not* have a lifestyle commensurate with my skillset.

That was the primary reason why I was still single. I was embarrassed of my situation. Not only that, but dating is expensive! Just going out for a drink or two with a date could easily add up to

$50. That was so far outside my daily budget, it wasn't even funny. When you have almost no income, you learn to live on virtually nothing. To give you an idea of how desperate things were back then, let me tell you about one particular situation.

I made a change in my daily routine starting on January 1st, 2005. Before that, I had gone to the gym in the evening and had always had a protein shake as my dinner. I'm a very routine-oriented person and had the same schedule every day. So as a matter of regular planning, I never had a reason to establish a dinner routine. It was unnecessary. The protein shake worked just fine. But at the beginning of 2005, I started going to the gym in the morning instead. It was a New Year's resolution, but it posed a problem. What would I have for dinner?

The meal had to be cheap and healthy. It also needed to be easy to prepare. I considered a variety of different options and decided on two chicken thighs, a baked yam and half a head of broccoli. I could bake the chicken thighs and the yam in a Pyrex pie plate at 375 for 30 minutes and then add the broccoli (with drizzled olive oil on top) for another 30 minutes. After one hour in the oven, my dinner would be ready.

All of the ingredients were cheap and the meal was quite healthy. It was perfect. I spent Christmas 2004 in Vancouver and flew back to San Francisco on December 30th. The next day, on New Year's Eve, I went to Costco and bought supplies. I bought two batches of chicken thighs and also got a jumbo box of Ziploc baggies. The box of Ziploc baggies actually contained four smaller boxes inside, each with 100 baggies inside. I put two chicken thighs in each baggie, making it easy for me to take one serving out each morning to defrost for dinner.

Almost a year later in December, 2005, I came back from another Costco run and started repackaging the chicken thighs into Ziploc baggies. Halfway through the batch, I finished my second box, and that's when it struck me. I'd had that dinner—two chicken thighs, a yam and half a head of broccoli—200 times during that year! The baggies were only used for that one purpose so the math hit me like a ton of bricks.

I hope this gives you an idea of my situation. Yes, I'm neurotic. I admit it. Yes, I'm obsessive. It's true. And yes, I can be extremely routine-oriented, but there was good reason for it all. I had no money. Period. I was so meticulous with my pennies that a $50 date with some woman was completely out of the question. I'm sure she would think nothing of it but for me, it represented a huge sacrifice.

I actually had an Excel spreadsheet with my daily food intake itemized in detail, including columns for protein, carbs and fat calories. Each meal was recorded, along with the cost of every single ingredient. My food intake was costing me $6.30 per day and it was perfectly balanced between protein, carbs and fat. A $50 date was equivalent to almost eight days of my regular diet. To do that was sabotaging my business and sabotaging my future.

The situation was frustrating beyond words. It messes with your head, actually. It threatened my manhood. I felt like a loser and yet, had no way of changing course. I was determined to become successfully self-employed and had bet the farm on that effort. I had no Plan B. Robert Strauss once said, "Success is like wrestling with a gorilla. You don't quit when you're tired. You quit when the gorilla is tired." I had no choice. I had to keep pushing.

NEW TECHNOLOGIES

I was watching the morning news on January 19th, 2006, just two days before my 36th birthday. I was still struggling to pay my bills and was desperate to make a change. The journalist was interviewing a "podcaster" about the Iraq war. A podcaster? What's that? I had heard that term but really had no idea what it meant. I looked it up on Google and discovered this emerging new technology.

I searched for the phrase "creating a podcast" and found a post describing the process in detail. I was desperate to make progress in my career. Maybe this was a way forward. Maybe this could help me succeed. The post recommended a specific microphone and a "pop filter" to smooth out the recording. It provided links to RSS hosting providers and various podcast directories.

For anyone who isn't that familiar with podcasts, they're most commonly downloaded from the iTunes music store. That's where you can download songs for 99¢ each but you can also download podcasts. Podcasts are essentially just audio recordings of a person's voice, usually teaching about a particular subject or interviewing someone. Think of it as talk radio. There are some video podcasts but the majority are audio.

I went to BestBuy and bought the recommended microphone and pop filter. I downloaded and installed the Audacity recording software as the post suggested. I opened an account on LibSyn.

com (which stands for Liberated Syndication) and was determined to upload my first podcast before bedtime.

During the previous year, 2005, I hosted workshops about the mortgage business. They were all about the complicated underwriting guidelines of these new Alt-A and subprime loan programs. I branded those workshops as my "Beyond the Rate" mortgage workshops because there are more important considerations when selecting a mortgage program than simply the interest rate. The terms can cost you far more than an eighth of a percentage point on the interest rate.

As a mortgage broker, my objective was obviously to attract new clients but it ended up being just one more failed marketing experiment. To promote the workshops, I bought print advertisements in the *Oakland Tribune* newspaper and held them at the Oakland Marriott hotel. It cost a fortune and the people who showed up were among the most destitute people I had ever met— even worse than me! One time, I had only eight people show up and the event cost over $2,000. I would've been better off standing on the street corner handing out $100 bills!

Anyway, I thought the podcast thing could be the perfect evolution of those workshops and since I had delivered the content many times before, I could quickly and easily write out the text for the audio lessons. I wrote out an introduction for the series and recorded it that afternoon. The MP3 file sounded good and I uploaded it to LibSyn.com and then registered the podcast on iTunes along with two or three other podcast directories. By 10:30 that same evening, I had my own podcast available on the Internet.

Six days later, after my meager birthday celebrations had come and gone, I wrote out the text and recorded my next episode, effectively the first lesson of my new "Beyond the Rate" podcast series, and uploaded it to LibSyn.com. The platform said that my first episode, the introduction, had been downloaded 17 times. 17 times? Who were these people? How did they find it? I hadn't told anyone about my little experiment and was shocked that 17 people had found it all on their own.

That's when things started to get interesting. I continued to record and publish additional episodes and watched as my audience started to grow. It was slow at first, but keep in mind that I recently had just eight people attend one of my live workshops and that cost me over $2,000. This new podcast wasn't costing me a dime and people were finding it all on their own. Even better, I suspected that the people who were finding me were intelligent and tech-savvy people.

The problem, of course, was that they weren't local. These people were all across the country and, in fact, even around the world. I had downloads in Holland and India. I had downloads in all 50 states. How could I monetize this effort? At one point, I was licensed in 38 different states, trying to chase the mortgage business from every obscure corner of the country. I once did a $38,750 refinance in Arkansas and made just $387 on the deal. It was a disaster.

In March, a website called MortgageDaily.com wrote a piece about my podcast series and the number of downloads spiked up. I was shocked. Not only had they found me but they liked my recordings enough that they recommended them to their own readers. In May, a company called Sparta Success in Connecticut, a real estate training company, recommended my series to their students. And then, in June, the big one hit. Justin Pritchard at About.com wrote a story about my series, and my audience exploded.

At that point, my "Beyond the Rate" podcast series was the third most popular finance-related podcast on iTunes and the #1 mortgage-related podcast. It was exciting but I still wasn't making any money. I had people calling me. I got emails. I chased a few pathetic deals here and there but my financial status hadn't changed one bit.

In the end, I recorded the introduction, 15 chapters and a conclusion to the series. That was another mistake. It never crossed my mind to keep it going. The emerging blogging culture was still brand new. I had an impressive and growing audience but had finished the project. I had taken my entire workshop (and much more, actually) and provided it in audio format. The resource was now complete. In hindsight, of course, I should've kept going. I should've positioned myself as the mortgage guru and found other ways to monetize, but I was clueless about that option at that time.

I uploaded my last episode, the conclusion, in July of 2006, just one month after the About.com article. And while the podcast's success was fun to talk about and fascinating for others to hear about, my situation remained unchanged. I was still broke with no better prospects of success than I had six months earlier.

If you start sharing content on the Internet and you start building an audience, don't stop! People will subscribe and follow your work if you publish new content on a regular basis. Podcasts are perfect for this, as are blogs and video blogs. Interview experts in your field, giving you endless content that delivers real value to your followers. I should've interviewed mortgage brokers, economics commentators and real estate agents but I never thought about that possibility back then.

Facilitating the conversation is just as valuable as *participating* in the conversation. By interviewing experts in your field, you're positioning yourself as an expert as well. You're acting as a conduit to the most valuable and relevant content. Your followers will rely on you to filter through all the noise and tell them what they need to know. Don't worry about being the expert at everything yourself. Instead, focus on *finding* expertise and then sharing it with your audience.

9

THE MORTGAGE MELTDOWN

Credit Card Balance: $7,336 (April, 2007)

I t was April 2007 when a press release announced that almost 20% of subprime mortgage holders were already in default. That sent shivers down Wall Street and the subprime mortgage tremors began. It would be another 18 months before the subprime mortgage problems ballooned into the full-blown financial crisis, but the media coverage began in mid-2007. Everyone wanted to talk about the mortgage meltdown, and there was simultaneously a fascination with podcasting. I was perfectly positioned.

I got called by a number of media outlets including the Associated Press (AP) and National Public Radio (NPR). It seemed insane to me that I was being treated as a subject matter expert on the problems shaking the financial world. I was just a struggling mortgage broker with a podcast on iTunes! The AP story was syndicated in 65 cities across the country and the NPR interview aired nationwide as well.

The media attention led to a handful of speaking inquiries; nothing big but it was new to me and I was excited about it. The topic was always the same: the subprime mortgage meltdown. But in one case, I got a call from someone asking if I could speak to their group but then said that he didn't want me to talk about real estate. "What would you like me to speak about?" I asked. "Podcasting." No kidding! This might be fun.

When I arrived at the group, the audience was full of young guys. That was rare for me. I was always speaking to older people, but not this time. These guys were young and they wanted marketing advice. I told them about my experience with podcasting and they were fired up. They loved it. They asked me all sorts of questions and I had all the answers they were looking for. I knew the topic from personal experience. I had done it all myself.

> Sometimes we forget about our own expertise. I never thought about the value of my podcasting expertise. I only thought about the value of my mortgage expertise, and my increasing expertise about the economic conundrum that the subprime crisis was creating. But my podcasting expertise was significant too. Think beyond your primary topic. Where else do you have expertise? What other value can you share?

I drove home that night thinking about how fun the event had been. I had a great time and felt really good about the value I shared. Those guys were mostly self-employed, just like me. They were trying to build businesses, just like me. I felt totally comfortable speaking about the podcasting topic because I had direct personal experience doing it myself.

Whenever I spoke about mortgages or the emerging financial crisis, I always felt uncomfortable. I didn't feel legitimate. I wasn't making tons of money and had never owned a home myself. What right did I have to talk about this subject? That wasn't a problem with podcasting. I had done it myself and the podcast had developed a respectable following. I decided that night that I would leave real estate behind and transition over to marketing.

THE LAW OF ATTRACTION

houghts become things. The Law of Attraction suggests that we manifest our futures with our own thoughts. If we think about something enough, it will manifest itself in our lives. The critics dismiss it as ridiculous, but the true distinction between credible and ridiculous is more subtle. The question is whether our thoughts are truly creative or not. Do we *create* with our thoughts? Or is the process simply a matter of probability combined with the power of the subconscious mind?

Researchers at the University of Pennsylvania and also at Neuro Focus (now part of the Nielsen Company) estimate that a person's subconscious mind makes as many as 10,000,000 observations in any given situation, ranging from the room temperature to the comfort of your seat to a scent in the air to a piece of lint on the floor. We notice everything, but not consciously. These observations are all made below our conscious awareness. By comparison, the average person can only keep track of about 40 *conscious* thoughts at one time.

Think about your current setting, reading this book. If you were instantly taken out of your current setting and then asked to describe it by memory, you could probably recount dozens and dozens of details easily. When you were in that setting, you probably didn't consciously make note of all those details, but they came in through your senses and were registered somewhere in your mind, easily accessed when someone asked you specifically about them.

The point is that you're not consciously aware of 99.99% of your observations. You are indeed making those observations. They come in through your eyes and your ears and your nose and your mouth. You just don't realize it, that's all. When I moved down to Los Angeles in 1998, I bought a dark green Volkswagen Jetta. As soon as I started driving it, I started noticing other Jettas everywhere around me. Has this happened to you too? It's a common phenomenon.

I was in sales at that time and spent my days driving those massive LA freeways. I'm sure I saw at least 10,000 cars each day. Were those Jettas there before I owned one myself? Did my thoughts *create* those Jettas? No, of course not. They were there the whole time, but I never noticed them before. This is the Law of Attraction (LOA) in action. It's not magic. It's probability.

By purposefully putting a focus in your mind, you will naturally start noticing things that are somehow related or consistent with that focus. If you focus on your challenges in life, you will see more of them and start believing that the world is a horrible place. If you focus on your blessings, you will see more of those too and start believing that the world is a wonderful place. If you're focused on building a business, you'll start noticing things that support that endeavor. If you want to move to Miami, you'll start noticing things that will help facilitate that move. And if you want to become a professional speaker like I did, you'll find countless things that end up leading you in that direction.

My life is the best example of the Law of Attraction that I have ever seen. When I started thinking about what I wanted to become, things seemed to automatically lead in that direction. Those mortgage workshops were a failure on their own, but they also led to the podcast series. The podcast series never generated any money but it led to the media exposure. The media exposure didn't generate any money either but it led to some of my early speaking opportunities. Even though my journey was lined with frustration and struggle, it was also going in precisely the right direction.

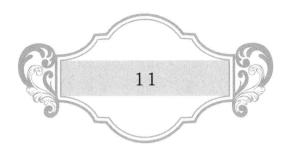

MY BROTHER'S WEDDING

My brother got married in August, 2006. He managed to secure an incredible location on the roof of a pavilion on Toronto's lakeside waterfront. It was so perfect for him. Growing up, Tom used to drive around Vancouver and inspect all the development posters at construction sites. He loved new buildings and innovative architecture. Here we were on this roof with Toronto's impressive skyline in the background. It was breathtaking.

His reception was at a different location and I was nervous. Tom had asked me to be his best man, a request I accepted happily. But now it was coming down to crunch time. We were sitting at the head table and the minutes were ticking down. I had to deliver my speech shortly and was looking out across the 150 people in attendance, including the rest of my own family. My stomach was in knots and two shots of tequila did almost nothing to calm my nerves.

I had worked hard on the speech. I bought two books about writing best-man speeches and even worked on it with Peter Hauck, a college friend from Ottawa. I even paid $17 for one of those online e-books with a bunch of wedding jokes. This was important to me. I love my brother very much and this was my first real opportunity to share my passion for speaking with my own family. I wanted to get it right.

Well, I did. I didn't bring the house down or anything, but it was a solid speech and the words came out of my mouth just as I had hoped. People even laughed at some of those jokes! And after dinner, a number of people came up to me and said nice things. I was so proud of what I had done and so happy to have contributed something positive to my brother's special day. You can read the speech here:

http://www.keynotemastery.com/wedding/

As a speaker, you can make a profound difference in people's lives. A well-written and well-delivered speech can directly impact the energy of an event, and your stories and insights are often remembered years later. What impact would *you* like to make? What insights would *you* like to share?

I spent almost two weeks in Toronto and as you might expect from a trip like that, it allowed me to look back at my own life with some perspective. On the flight home, I turned on my laptop and opened Microsoft Excel. Thoughts were racing through my mind. I was returning to my regular life and wanted to make some changes. I had been self-employed for almost four years at that point and was still struggling to pay my bills.

I started listing all the good qualities I had, each one in a different row. The list included everything from salsa dancing and weightlifting to conceptual thinking and business acumen. And surprise, surprise, public speaking was on that list as well. In the next three columns, I added possible uses for each quality. The exercise was really interesting because I soon realized that I could easily spend my whole life doing *only* things I'm good at. With 11 qualities and two or three uses for each one, I could build my entire life around those strong qualities.

Visit **Keynote**Mastery.com to download worksheet #1 to do this exercise yourself.

JOINING TOASTMASTERS

The first practical application of my public speaking quality was to join Toastmasters. I visited a club in Vancouver about a decade earlier but was unimpressed with the group. There were a bunch of odd characters in the room and it seemed like amateur night to me. I had made no special contributions that evening but ended up winning the "best speaker of the night" ribbon at the end. I certainly didn't feel like I could learn anything from that group and never went back. But at this point, I thought it was worth a second shot.

During the following two weeks, I visited six different Toastmasters clubs near my home. I was unimpressed with the first five but enjoyed the sixth. It was the Lamorinda Toastmasters Club and one of its members was a young bald guy who looked like he was in great shape physically. Most Toastmasters members are older. It's rare to find someone in their 20s or 30s, so this guy stuck out to me right away. With someone else roughly my own age, I felt more comfortable and joined the following week.

Toastmasters has speaking contests in the spring and fall of each year. I decided to compete in the spring contest and wrote a speech entitled "Deliberate Curiosity" for the occasion. It was all about staying curious and appreciating that everybody in the world is better at *something* than you are. Everybody has some skill that you don't have yourself and as a result, you can learn from everyone. It had a positive thought-provoking angle which worked perfectly for the contest format. You can read it here:

http://www.keynotemastery.com/toastmasters/

The spring contest also included an evaluation contest where the contestants all hear one canned speech and then compete by providing evaluations for the speaker. The best evaluation wins. There's an art to it and the applications in business and management are obvious. I competed in both categories.

I delivered the speech well and won the first prize in both categories at my club, advancing to the "area" contest. This was the beginning of an amazing run. I competed at the area and won both categories there too, advancing to the division level. I competed and won first prize in both categories again. Six first-prize awards so far! The next level was the twice-yearly Toastmasters District 57 conference. I would be speaking in an auditorium with over 300 people in attendance!

Within the Toastmasters universe, the District Conference is a big deal. The Toastmasters organization relies heavily on a volunteer leadership structure that is elected at every level (club, area, division and district) each year. Some of the members are extremely active and are treated with a lot of respect from other members. It's quite possible to be a big fish in the Toastmasters pond, and all these big fish attend the District Conferences.

Since I had won at the division level, a couple of the bigger clubs invited me to deliver my speech at their clubs. It was presented as an opportunity for me to practice my speech. I was representing the entire division at the District Conference and the big fish wanted to ensure I was ready for the fight. The whole thing was a little strange for me. I had been a member for less than six months at that point and definitely felt flattered by all the attention but also didn't expect the pressure that came along with it.

I was given a series of CDs filled with winning speeches from the World Champion of Public Speaking finale at the once-annual Toastmasters International Convention. The speeches were dynamic, funny and inspiring. Craig Valentine, the world champion from 1999, was on one of those CDs and he was also scheduled to be the keynote speaker at the District Conference. I would meet him in person—a real live professional speaker!

The winner of the World Champion of Public Speaking prize becomes an instant celebrity in the Toastmasters world. Many Toastmasters members, either secretly or otherwise, yearn to reach those heights; the winning speaker immediately becomes an idol within the community. In fact, the amount of attention is enough to propel them into a full-time speaking career if they wish to embrace that path.

For me, the opportunity was unrivaled. This contest might launch my career as a professional speaker. This was my chance. This could be my indisputable victory, my undeniable achievement. This could be my justification to speak in front of audiences around the world.

Craig Valentine's keynote was the first scheduled event of the day, and he was amazing. He was dynamic and funny. His speech was inspiring and thought-provoking. There were no ah's and um's. He used pauses brilliantly. The timing was perfect. But none of those things caught my attention as much as one word: Dubai. During his speech, Craig mentioned that he had spoken in Dubai. Dubai! I couldn't believe it. What would it be like to speak in such an exotic city?

Dubai was the most exotic destination that I could imagine. It was the thriving new metropolis in the United Arab Emirates, an experiment in urban development never before undertaken in the Muslim world. The Arab nations had tons of money from oil sales but they had never invested that money in their own world before. They had always invested it in Japanese, European and American assets. But starting in the early 90s, Arab nations started investing in Dubai and the development boom had taken the region by storm. At one point, over 25% of the world's construction cranes (over 30,000 in total) were operating simultaneously in Dubai. The thought that Craig Valentine had spoken there blew my mind. If that wasn't the pinnacle of professional speaking, I didn't know what was.

The evaluation contest was just before lunch and the speech contest—the main event—was during the afternoon. I could hardly eat my lunch and felt nauseous afterward. My nerves were a mess. The auditorium was big, with theater-style seating. Bright lights made it almost impossible to see the audience from the stage. Even still, when I was finally introduced and walked onto that stage, I was painfully aware of the 300 people sitting right in front of me.

I stood there for four or five seconds before saying anything. It was an unnatural silence but the rules state that the clock doesn't start until the speaker begins speaking, so I took my time. I took one more deep breath and launched into my speech. My biggest fear was that I would forget the words. I've never been good at memorization, but was forced to do so here because of the strict time limits. If my speech was longer than seven minutes and 30 seconds, I would be disqualified. During my practice sessions, I regularly came in at 7:15 or 7:20, so it was essential that I stuck to my script.

The words came out perfectly. My mind stayed clear. My "Deliberate Curiosity" topic was different from that of the other contestants, and I explained the concept with the passion of a loving father speaking to his child. The speech clocked in at 7:27 and I stood there with enormous pride as applause poured out from the darkness. Regardless of the final outcome, this was a huge accomplishment. For those seven minutes, I truly felt like a speaker.

The second-place winner is always announced first. It wasn't me. And the first place winner? Well, that wasn't me either. My run was over. I did, however, win first place in the evaluation contest, but that category doesn't advance beyond the district level. I was definitely disappointed that my dreams of becoming the 2007 World Champion of Public Speaking had evaporated, but I represented my division respectably and met tons of new people in the process. I still have the trophy displayed in my office, but the primary impact of the whole experience was Craig's Dubai reference. That word was seared into my brain and I was determined to get there one day as well.

Toastmasters is an amazing place to hone your speaking skills. It will help you cultivate awareness of various speaking techniques. Darren LaCroix, the 2001 World Champion of Public Speaking, says the key to becoming an effective speaker is "stage time, stage time, stage time" and I couldn't agree more. I would recommend Toastmasters to any aspiring keynote speaker.

MOM, DAD AND MEETUP.COM

During the contest season, I met a guy from another club who was the organizer of a group of Law of Attraction advocates and he invited me to attend one of his events. It was held at a local restaurant and I was shocked to find over 30 people in attendance. Who was this guy? And how did he have such a large following? My curiosity was piqued.

After the meeting was over, I asked one of the other attendees how she had heard about the event. She said it was listed on Meetup.com. I had never heard of that site before but checked it out as soon as I got home. I was fascinated by the platform and joined a variety of different groups that evening, mostly in the business and entrepreneurial categories. One of them was called the East Bay Entrepreneur Meetup.

About a month after that night, the organizer for the East Bay Entrepreneur Meetup stepped down and the platform opened the organizer role up to any of the existing members. I remember sitting in front of my computer as the email popped into my inbox. Should I take it? The group had about 180 members and I immediately felt nervous, as if I were about to do something wrong. I stared at the email and hovered my mouse over the link, wondering if this would somehow get me into trouble. Eventually I held my breath and clicked on the link. A few seconds later, I was officially the new organizer. Did anyone notice? I had no idea.

I started looking for places where I could hold a meeting. There was a restaurant in Walnut Creek that had a side room that I could rent for $50, so that's what I did. I posted the new event on the group's calendar and sent an email announcement to the members. The event was scheduled for a Thursday evening in July and I was excited to meet my members. My very first meeting with that group would be as their leader!

When that week arrived, I attended my weekly Toastmasters meeting on Tuesday evening, just two days before my first meeting with the Meetup group. I parked my car and was walking towards the building when my cell phone rang. It was my mother in Vancouver. That phone call ushered in the worst two years of my life.

Credit Card Balance: $12,963 (July, 2007)

My mother has serious psychological problems. She has borderline personality disorder and gets confused, anxious and angry when she can't control her environment. She also had a brain tumor that was removed in 1999. They opened her skull for the operation and although we never got any official assessment, it didn't seem to go well. Her primary symptom before the operation was persistent buzzing in her head and it never went away afterward. Meanwhile, her nerve endings didn't grow back properly and she was left with half of her face sagging and a deep impression by her right temple.

Meanwhile, my dad was diagnosed with Parkinson's disease in 2005 (when he was 70 years old)and the medication was well known to cause constipation. He managed the situation fairly well with laxatives but eventually, his system backed up so badly that it was essentially poisoning him from the inside out. He ended up in bed, unable to get up and leaking from behind. He had now been stuck in bed for over 24 hours.

It was unpleasant and stank like sewage. My mother couldn't make sense of it anymore and freaked out. She told me that there was a farm animal in her bed. It was my dad. She honestly thought my father was a farm animal. She was hysterical and couldn't put a proper sentence together. I begged her to give the phone to the animal but she refused. I asked her if she had given him any food. She said no. I could feel that swelling, crying sensation creeping up my throat. I pleaded with her to give the phone to the animal and she finally agreed.

"She thinks you're an animal, dad," I said.

"Yeah, I know," he whispered. I could hardly hear his voice. He had no energy at all.

We've had dementia-related episodes with my mother before but this was the worst by far. The situation was awful but for me, there was an ironic silver lining. She was intensely critical of me when I was a teenager. "You're on the road to hell." "You'll never amount to anything." I heard those statements regularly and they fueled my intellectual insecurities. But when she was finally diagnosed with borderline personality disorder, it took the weight out of her judgments. I was vindicated. After all, she was mentally ill. Her diagnosis helped me dismantle those limiting beliefs and build confidence in my own individuality.

Limiting beliefs are killers. They destroy your sense of self-worth and cause you to sabotage opportunities when they arise. My mother has endured enormous suffering at the hands of her illness but her diagnosis was a blessing in disguise for me. It allowed me to put her temper tantrums into context and quiet my inner critic. Who was critical of *you*? Who fueled *your* limiting beliefs? Perhaps those critiques stemmed from fear or insecurity. Perhaps they were a result of mental illness. Perhaps it's time to put those judgments aside and adopt more empowering beliefs.

The immediate problem was that we couldn't leave my mother alone. Ever since 2006, she couldn't function on her own anymore. She would freak out and have no idea what to do. So if an ambulance came to get my dad, she would be alone. While still on the phone, I begged her to give the farm animal some orange juice and she eventually did. In the morning, we called an ambulance and arranged for some family friends to pick up my mother and take care of her for the day. I would arrive in Vancouver by early afternoon.

Shortly after I arrived, my mother was brought back to the house by her friends. She was happy and had no idea that anything was wrong. With her dementia, once the immediate crisis passed, she immediately forgot everything that had happened. Meanwhile, the house was a mess. The bed sheet had been stuffed into the toilet and everything seemed unkempt and dirty. My mom didn't even seem to notice. We gathered a few things and drove to the hospital.

Walking into my dad's hospital room was overwhelming. Before that day, I hadn't cried in over 10 years and often wondered if I somehow lacked the capacity for emotion. Was I a robot? I do have feelings, lots of them, but they never brought tears to my eyes. I wasn't trying to bury anything. I just never really felt emotions, that's all. Anyway, my mother and I walked into my dad's room and I saw him there with an IV in his arm. He looked weak and defeated.

My dad was a saint. With my mother's psychological problems, he had put up with *soooo* much over the years. When my mother would go on one of her rampages, the four of us kids would go downstairs and wait for the madness to pass, but my father would stay up there and try to calm her down. She would yell and cry, and he would wait patiently for her to unwind.

Someone once told me that the mood swings with bipolar disorder last for weeks, while the mood swings with borderline personality disorder last for hours. That was generally true with my mom. You could tell when it was coming. She would stop talking (the silent treatment) and the mood in the house would get increasingly tense over the course of three or four days. Eventually, something would set her off and she would start freaking out. Sometimes, she would even hit you with her hands. It never hurt but the anger and rage would be so intense in her eyes that I would shake for hours afterward.

Despite these regular outbursts, my dad loved her. He was completely devoted to her. He grew up in a blue-collar household in Philadelphia and yearned for a more cultured lifestyle. He put himself through university, eventually earning his PhD from Notre Dame, and then went to Switzerland for his post-doc. That's where he met my mother. She was from an aristocratic family and was the picture of European culture.

My mother was my dad's ticket to a better life. He was a highly intelligent and gentle man. He wrote poetry and appreciated the opera and classical music, and he knew he had met his dream girl. My mother was the center of his world. If you met her, you would think she was a sweet and well-educated Swiss woman, and she was, but she had a viciously cruel side that she saved for those she loved most; her own family. Even still, my dad stood up for her no matter what.

Less than a day earlier, she had had one of her rampages and treated him like a farm animal, not even knowing what she was doing. And yet again, he took the abuse without hesitation. Of course, in this case, he had no choice but even if he did, he would've stood by her with as much love and compassion as he had thirty years earlier.

I took one look at my dad and my face exploded into tears. I couldn't even speak. The water gushed out of my eyes so quickly that it almost immediately started dripping from my chin. I sat on his hospital bed beside him and held his hand. I was a mess and couldn't get a single word out. He responded by crying himself and my mother stood there, completely unemotional, like someone watching a movie of people she didn't even know. She was so confused by everything. She had no idea what was going on.

Growing up, my dad never expressed his emotions. I never heard him yell and I never saw him cry. But when he was diagnosed with Parkinson's disease, the medication had two main side effects. First, it caused constipation, which is what resulted in this particular situation, but it also made him more emotional. He cried easily now, both in sadness and in joy. Almost anything would make him cry and it frustrated him. He would often interrupt his own crying and blame the medication. I wasn't surprised when he cried in the hospital but he was surprised that I did, especially with the intensity that I had that day.

Later that evening, I spoke with my sister, Denise, on the phone and again broke down in tears. After that, I spoke with a friend, Gina, down in San Francisco and it happened again: hot uncontrollable tears. I had cried three times in one day. As much as my heart ached with the situation unfolding in front of me, I was also relieved that I was reacting this way. The appropriate response was to cry and that's what I was doing. It made me feel normal. It made me feel human.

Talking to Gina reminded me that I had my East Bay Entrepreneur meeting on the following evening. I knew I had to get someone to facilitate the meeting and Gina was the perfect person for the job. I also called Josh and another friend, John, and the three of them went to the restaurant and ran the meeting. It seemed crazy to me that I didn't even attend my first meeting, but that group ended up defining my life for the following three years.

SWEDEN IN THE WINTER

Credit Card Balance: $14,853 (September, 2007)

I was drinking a Corona at my desk two months later. It was a Thursday evening in September. My new Meetup group was just getting started. I wasn't making any money on mortgages anymore and had yet to gain any real traction on the marketing business. My credit card debts were mounting and I didn't know what to do. I sat there frantically brainstorming what I might do to kick-start my business.

When I was still working for Pimlico Apparel in Vancouver, Gary Lennett, one of the two brothers who owned the company and I prepared and delivered a session entitled "Survivors at Retail: Powerful Insights for the Future of Promotional Wearables" during the "education day" at the 1997 Promotional Products Association International (PPAI) annual trade show in Dallas. We had over 600 attendees and it went extremely well. We were asked to return the following year and deliver the same session again. It was one of the most exciting and rewarding things I had ever done, and it was my one and only experience speaking at a conference.

I should try to speak at another conference! I searched for the phrase "Internet marketing conference" on Google. "Internet marketing" was the keyword phrase that encompassed all the new digital-marketing channels. It turned out that there actually *was* an Internet Marketing Conference (IMC) and the website came up first in the search results. I visited the website and the upcoming conference featured on the homepage was scheduled to take place two months later, November, in Stockholm, Sweden.

My first reaction was to immediately dismiss the idea and look for other conferences. It was ridiculous to think I could speak at a conference in Sweden when I had yet to cover my new digital-marketing topic at an American conference. But I spent an extra few seconds looking at the site and clicked on the Speakers tab. There were a series of additional details outlined on that page and at the bottom, a link to *Submit a Proposal*. I clicked on that link as well.

At this point, I was staring at an online form for prospective speakers to fill out to propose a session. Should I fill this out? I felt a surge of nervous energy shoot up my spine similar to the feeling I had when becoming the organizer of the East Bay Entrepreneur Meetup. I took another gulp from my Corona and started looking at the questions. The form requested information about the speaker, contact information and website and then focused on the proposed session title and description. Ideas started swirling through my head.

When I started my podcast, I got to know a few of the other emerging podcasters on iTunes. And when you're a single guy, it's inevitable that you do a search or two for women-related topics. Lo and behold, I found "The Pick-up Podcast" with AJ and Jordan. Little did I know, after pornography and gambling, the "seduction community" is one of the most vibrant niches on the Internet—there were countless gurus giving guys advice on how to meet women.

"The Pick-up Podcast" was awesome! They did interviews with various "experts" and talked about women and the "cold approach pick-up." They were all hysterically funny and the content was fascinating. I used to download the episodes and listen to them while working out at the gym. I loved it. Anyway, I listened to one interview with a guy who was focused on advancing interactions with women from rapport to romance. How do you avoid the "friend zone" by projecting masculine sexual energy at the beginning of new relationships?

I loved the alliteration of *rapport to romance* and with the Corona flowing through my veins, I thought of other angles on the same concept. I came up with a title that evening that was one of the best titles I've ever crafted. In the speaking business, compelling titles and descriptions are extremely important. The title I thought of that night was:

"Monetizing Trust: Leading Your Audience from Rapport to Revenue"

It was a killer title. I pieced together an equally dynamic description, drank some more Corona and clicked *submit*. I never expected to hear back. I hadn't published any books and had no indisputable victories in my past. My podcast series and my Entrepreneur Meetup were the only real successes I had. And true to my expectations, I heard nothing on the following day, Friday, nothing on Saturday and nothing on Sunday. But on Monday morning, I woke up and found an email in my inbox. It had come in at about 2:00 AM, which was 10:00 AM in Sweden. "We're interested in your proposal."

The anxiety shot through my body like an electric shock. It took me at least an hour to calm down enough to respond to their email. They asked a few questions in their email and I did my best to provide useful answers. The emails started going back and forth and it looked like they might indeed invite me to speak at their conference. I was pinching myself daily, waiting for their email replies to arrive.

Eventually, the line went quiet. Their replies stopped coming in. What happened? I was panicking inside. I didn't want the fantasy to disappear. I didn't want to lose this opportunity. After a day or two of waiting, I sent them an email explaining that I had already begun my travel plans and needed to hear back from them in order to proceed. They replied and told me that their schedule had filled up and they no longer had room for my session.

No way! I wasn't about to let this fantasy get wiped off the map that easily. I sent another email and basically begged them to keep me on the agenda. I offered to pay for my own travel and requested no speaker fee whatsoever. That's right. I offered to do the whole thing for free. I hated doing it but had no other choice. If I didn't offer up the farm, the opportunity would vanish forever.

The next day, they replied and told me they would keep me on the agenda but that my speaking slot would only be 12 minutes long. That's insane. I had enough frequent flyer points to get my flight for free but the taxes on the flight were still over $100 and the hotel would cost me at least $400 more. Everything was expensive over there and it would basically wipe me out financially, and all for a 12-minute speaking slot? It was a crazy gamble.

The only thing I kept thinking about was the fact that I would be speaking at a conference in Sweden. It seemed so exotic. It seemed so implausible. I *had* to make it happen! I *had* to give it a shot. Before replying to their email, I called United Mileage Plus and booked my flight. I then made reservations at the Crowne Plaza Hotel in downtown Stockholm, and then replied to their email and agreed to their terms. I also included all of my travel reservations to ensure they understood that I was serious about my intentions. They confirmed the next day.

Credit Card Balance: $20,289 (November, 2007)

It's difficult to explain exactly how terrified I was. I suppose I could describe how my digestive tract was functioning during my flight over to Sweden, but that probably wouldn't be appropriate for a book like this. Suffice it to say, I was scared to death. I felt like a gladiator entering a ring full of lions and tigers. What in the world had I gotten myself into? Was I about to make a fool of myself on an international stage? I was petrified.

I don't sleep well on planes to begin with, and being scared stiff obviously made it worse, so there was no hope for any z's on the flight. The person sitting beside me on the connecting flight from Heathrow to Stockholm told me that the easiest way to adjust to the time change is to stay awake as long as possible and try to go to bed at the normal bed time in Stockholm, sleep through the night and that I should be fine the next day. At least that's what she claimed.

The event was in late November and Stockholm is roughly at the same latitude as Anchorage (59 degrees versus 61 degrees), so the sun went down around 3:00 PM. I took a walk through the snowy streets of downtown Stockholm and eventually crashed around 6:00 PM. I woke up at 2:00 AM to the sound of drunken revelers walking down the street after a long night of partying, singing songs I didn't understand. I was wide awake and the hotel restaurant didn't open until 6:00 AM.

After going through my PowerPoint slides for the millionth time and doing pushups and standing squats for a couple of hours, I took a shower and slowly got myself ready for the day. My stomach was still in knots but my bowels were completely empty. I was standing outside the restaurant door when it opened at 6:00 AM and was at the conference location, just two blocks down the road, by 7:15. None of the attendees had arrived yet but a few of the organizers were already there setting things up for the day.

I met the Executive Director for the conference, Lennart Svanberg. He was a bit shorter than me and had a very matter-of-fact demeanor. He showed me to a large room with a stage at the front and a large screen overhead. Other people slowly started arriving but I had no idea what to say to them. I didn't know how to introduce myself or explain what I did for a living. I was still trying to figure that out myself.

The whole thing was very awkward. I just wanted the sessions to begin so I could get an idea of what this would all look like. Aside from the two PPAI conferences in Dallas, this was the first conference I had ever spoken at. My session was scheduled for the afternoon, so I would hear at least five or six speakers before my turn came up. I managed to speak to almost no one before the conference started.

There were two things that struck me immediately when the sessions began. First, the speakers were extremely boring and seemed very uncomfortable on stage. You don't realize the dynamism of American speakers until you go elsewhere. There's a true showmanship culture in America and it's on full display in any type of performance environment, including professional speaking. American speakers are more dynamic and entertaining.

Of course, the Europeans often look down at this quality. Just like my own mother, they value people who are cultured and refined, and the Americans don't qualify. My mother hates the United States. She always has. It's a country of uncultured barbarians and her view is not uncommon in Europe. Nevertheless, the cultured and refined speakers in Stockholm that day made drying paint look exciting.

The second thing I noticed was that their presentations were far more technical than my own. Despite being boring, these people were working with real software platforms and their presentations were designed to share their developments and their findings with the other attendees. My presentation had no such technical prowess. It was a conceptual presentation about sharing valuable content to build trust before trying to sell stuff. I even had a photo of an engagement ring on one of my slides, representing the trust that can be earned by delivering value consistently. Nobody else was showing engagement rings!

When my session finally arrived, I was nervous beyond words, but I felt this intense feeling of resignation. I had to forget about the fact that my presentation was completely different from the others. I had to resign myself to the fact that my session would fall outside the standard format. I had to push through the awkwardness and deliver my presentation with passion and conviction. As they say in football, I had to leave it all on the field.

I'm good at public speaking. I've known it since I was young. My presentation style is engaging and dynamic. I genuinely try to help attendees see a new paradigm and consider the value of an entirely new perspective. It's almost as if I'm speaking to a young child and explaining the world with all the love of a father or grandparent. My presentations are always that way and this one was no exception.

Years later, after contributing to multiple events Lennart organized around the world, he admitted to me that he thought my presentation had almost no content at all. He told me that he couldn't believe I would travel across the world to show people photos of engagement rings. But I had received the second-highest rating of all the speakers at that 2007 Stockholm conference. I had delivered my empty content with the dynamism of a real American speaker and the attendees loved it. It was the beginning of a fruitful business relationship.

That evening, a number of the attendees went to the bar in my hotel for a drink. The Swedish people love to drink. I ordered a beer and it was 95 krona. In 2007, that was about $16 USD for one beer! I was spending money I didn't have, but I needed the drink as much as any drink I've ever had in my whole life and didn't hesitate. Lennart hadn't talked to me much at that point but he made an effort to come over and start a conversation, and I was grateful.

After a few initial pleasantries, he told me that the primary reason he invited me to the conference was because I'm an American from Silicon Valley. Are you kidding me? First of all, I live in Walnut Creek, which is an hour drive away from Silicon Valley. And secondly, by that loose geographic definition, there are over seven million people who qualify. There's nothing particularly special about where I live but in Sweden, it was apparently something special.

Think about your assets. This is an asset I never knew I had. I'm an American from Silicon Valley and that has value in international markets. Who knew? Seriously, think about your assets. Maybe you're a man. That's an asset for some markets. Maybe you're a woman. That's an asset in different markets. Maybe you speak English. Maybe you speak Spanish or Mandarin. Maybe you're from India or Brazil. Maybe you have a sexy British accent. These are all things that can be leveraged in the right circumstances.

Would you like to know what else he told me? He told me that I was the only American who submitted a proposal! No kidding. That's incredible. So by going to the other side of the world, I had effectively *eliminated* my competition! I had no competitors. None. It blew my mind.

Just think about it for a moment. I got credibility in Sweden because I was an American from Silicon Valley. And then when I got back home, I got credibility here because I had spoken professionally in Sweden! The adventure gave me credibility in both directions. I had a built-in advantage flying over there, and I had an advantage flying back home too.

That was the whole point. The only reason I splurged my measly savings on this trip was because I wanted to add the experience to my resume. I wanted to say that I had spoken at a conference in Sweden. That was my primary objective, and now it turned out that I had a competitive advantage when applying to speak at international events. I was sold. When I got back home, I started researching conferences in every exotic corner of the globe and sending my marketing materials to every single one of them.

This trip was the beginning of my "hack" as a professional speaker. I sent envelopes to Kuala Lumpur and Abu Dhabi and

Santiago, Chile. I sent envelopes to Moscow and Bangkok and Cape Town. I sent them everywhere. One year, I spent almost $6,000 on postage. It was the primary focus of my marketing efforts.

I worked like crazy to secure these exotic international events because it was building my credibility here at home. This was the beginning of my *think bigger* mentality that would later become my signature message as a speaker. Why would I spin my wheels chasing the same goals as everyone else, goals which are just a tiny bit bigger than last year's goal? Why not shoot for the big goal, the one that's 10 times bigger than anyone else is shooting for? If I shoot for the bigger one, I'd have no competition. It would literally be easier to shoot for the huge goals than to compete with the rest of the pack.

GETTING TO THE TOP

There's a metaphor that I've carried around with me for years now. Every career is like a skyscraper. Real estate is a skyscraper. Insurance is another skyscraper. Politics, manufacturing, retail, they're all individual skyscrapers. And some are taller than others. Politics, for example, is really tall and right at the top is the President of the United States. That's the highest office in that skyscraper.

Regardless of which skyscraper you're in, the question is always the same: what's the fastest way to the top? Ambitious people always want to get to the top of their fields. So what's the fast way up? The first option is to take the stairs, and it works. It takes a long time. It's difficult. But you will eventually get there. Imagine someone who starts in the mailroom and after 35 years with the company, ends up becoming the CEO. That happens from time to time. Those stories are real.

A faster way up is to take the elevators, and that works too. It'll get you to the top a lot faster. Imagine someone who goes to Harvard or Yale and becomes CEO in 15 or 20 years. That happens quite a bit. Most Fortune 500 CEOs went to Ivy League schools and became CEOs in this way. They took the elevators. But the fastest way to get to the top floor of a skyscraper isn't either of these ways. The fastest way to get to the top floor of a skyscraper is to parachute down onto it from above.

I believe this is possible today. In today's connected digital world, I believe it's possible to metaphorically parachute down onto your goals from above. If you think bigger and just start doing the things that the superstars are doing, you can literally become that person yourself. The process becomes the reality. It's actually a very natural progression.

Now, just to be clear, I'm not talking about thinking just a *little* bit bigger. That doesn't work. I'm talking about thinking *way* bigger—like, 10 times bigger or even 100 times bigger! If you do *that* and if you take massive action in that direction, you can literally come down onto your goals from above. I believe that's possible today and frankly, it's the story of my own life.

Think bigger. It's not just an empty phrase. It's as real for me as anything I've ever experienced. And if it can work this way for me, it can work this way for you too. The only reason my speaking career came together is because I went for the big opportunities, accidentally at first. They never would've hired me if I were a local Stockholm guy. And nobody was hiring me back home because there were a thousand other guys just like me.

You can never be a prophet in your own land. By going far away, I was able to leverage an advantage that I didn't have back home. If I chased little goals, I'm not sure I would've made it. But because of this serendipitous experience, started with zero expectations over a Corona one Thursday evening, my life began to change and I started to realize the power of thinking bigger. I finally began to realize the allure of big, huge, massively audacious goals.

THINKING BIGGER

More and more, I started incorporating this theme into my speaking programs. Years later, when I started my video blog, I finished each video with the phrase: "Think bigger about your business. Think bigger about your life!" It became a mantra for me and I thought about it constantly. I bought books like *Think and Grow Rich* by Napoleon Hill, *The 10x Rule* by Grant Cardone and *The Magic of Thinking Big* by David J. Schwartz. I was constantly on the lookout for other people's thoughts and ideas on the subject, and a structure started to take shape.

There's an interesting domino effect that begins when you think bigger. In particular, three things tend to happen. First, your life is simply more exciting. People who have big goals are generally happier than those who have small goals. In fact, the evolving science of happiness always identifies *purpose* as an essential ingredient. People want to have a purpose. They want to be part of something bigger than just themselves. And what does that sound like? It sounds like having ambitious and audacious goals.

The research also shows that happy people consistently perform better than their unhappy counterparts. In research described by Shawn Achor in *The Happiness Advantage*, happy employees were more productive, happy doctors were faster and more accurate and happy salespeople sold more. So by thinking bigger, people are happier and then, as a result, tend to perform better. It's a massive self-fulfilling prophecy. By thinking bigger, you immediately increase the chances of achieving that goal.

The second thing that happens is that you inspire everyone else around you including your employees, your customers and even your suppliers. Everyone wants to be part of the big thing. When you're working on a big ambitious goal, everyone else gets a bit jealous and wants to be a part of it themselves. In *Bold: How to Go Big, Make Bank, and Better the World,* Peter Diamandis and Steven Kotler talk about the strategy of isolating teams of people to work on big projects. It immediately improves performance because the individual team members are energized by being part of something special.

Yet again, thinking bigger becomes a self-fulfilling prophecy because the moment you announce the goal, voluntary supporters start coming out of the woodwork. People get inspired by your vision and ambition and want to be a part of it, helping you achieve it in the process. Of course, you can't be selfish about it. You have to be willing to let other people play a meaningful role, but the net effect is that you get the wheels in motion towards the goal's achievement.

Finally, thinking bigger often results in less competition because everyone else is too busy chasing "realistic" goals. Screw realistic goals! I'm not saying it's going to work every time. Success is never guaranteed. But why chase the same goal that everyone else is chasing, the one that's just a little bit higher than last year's performance? I'll shoot for the big one! You may as well shoot for the big one because you might just surprise yourself. You might be the only one there, making it happen all on your own.

I'm not suggesting you eliminate all of your realistic goals. By all means, keep them in place but add a few big ones to the list. Add a homerun goal to the list. Take a shot at something truly remarkable. Take a shot at something big. In my experience, you won't run up against much competition at all. If anything, you'll inspire your competition and they might want to join your team.

Visit **Keynote**Mastery.com to download worksheet #2 on thinking bigger.

62

Taking Action

T his is one of the most important concepts in my life. I've been on this journey for a long time and have learned many things along the way, but this one concept has emerged as my core belief. The road to *being* is through *doing*. If you want to *be* happy, you need to *do* happy. If you want to *be* healthy, you need to *do* healthy. And if you want to *be* successful, you need to *do* successful! You need to find the people that are already successful in your industry and *do* the same things that they're doing.

Seriously, the simplicity of this is deceptive. I worked like crazy and spent all my savings to go to Sweden but as soon as I got back home, I *became* the guy who spoke in Sweden! As soon as I finished the task, it became part of my bio. I added references to the trip to my website. It became part of my marketing message. And when I later went to Dubai and Bangkok and Moscow, I added those to my bio as well. It didn't matter where I went, I added each trip to my online identity and people started treating me as if I had done all those things. Why? Because I had.

People will treat you consistently with the things they know about you. When a woman walks into the room and your colleague tells you she's the top salesperson in the company, you treat her differently than you would if she was just an ordinary person. When someone walks in and you hear that he's a billionaire, you treat him differently. It's natural. As human beings, we do this automatically. Meanwhile, those expectations end up giving those people enormous advantages to perpetuate their own success. It's a lot easier to act like James Bond when everyone *expects* you to act like James Bond.

The key is to focus on *doing*. Do stuff. Tony Robbins often talks about taking massive action and he's right. Pretend you're already that super-successful person and then do the things that that type of person would be doing. Imagine what someone at the top of your industry would be doing with his or her time. Now do those same things yourself. Put yourself into the role and the process becomes the reality. Doing those things makes you actually become that person.

Keep in mind that these realizations came to me during a time when I was still struggling. My evolving mindset didn't change my reality very quickly, as you'll soon see, but the clouds were clearing in my mind. I started to see how these things actually work in practice. Although I didn't actually read *The Secret* until 2010, this was The Law of Attraction in action. By focusing on a particular end result and acting like I was already there, my life was shifting towards that destination.

Visit **Keynote**Mastery.com to download worksheet #3 on taking action.

CHRISTMAS, 2007

I got back from Sweden victorious. It was now early December and my mind had exploded while I was away. It seemed the potential was endless. I had turned a corner and was excited to begin my new marketing plan after the holidays. But in the meantime, since I was the closest sibling to Vancouver and since I was the only one who wasn't married and had no kids, I had committed to visiting my parents for the holidays.

Since the meltdown in the summer, we had managed to get 24-hour care into the house. It was obvious that my parents needed it, but my mother hated those caregivers. She hated them with a passion. She didn't like the invasion of privacy and felt threatened when the female caregivers would care for my dad. I could tell from the phone calls that the tension was skyrocketing and although I wasn't there to witness them, I was sure the rampages were continuing as well.

To make matters worse, a nurse was visiting the house every second day to clean my dad's bedsores. He was in the hospital for almost a month during the summer and infected sores had formed on both heels. At one point, the infection got into his bones and things got critical but with regular cleanings, the situation had stabilized. When the wound was cleaned, you could still see his bone in the opening.

All the while, he was stuck in his wheelchair, completely unable to buffer my mother from the real world. He believed that was his primary mission at this stage in their marriage and felt guilty because he couldn't keep her "on the rails" as well as he did before. A year later when the situation had digressed further, he told me that he thought the whole thing was his fault. If he could buffer my mother's mania, everything would still be fine. Bullshit! My dad was a saint and believe me, none of this was his fault. None of it.

Anyway, my mother of course hated the nurses as well. She believes she's better than everybody else and doesn't fare well when others infringe on her territory. That was happening every day now and her moods were volatile, to say the least. When I entered the front door, she was screaming at one of the caregivers while my dad sat despondent in his wheelchair having his wounds cleaned. There were no Christmas decorations anywhere and I immediately felt that crying instinct press up my throat again.

I tried to act light and almost playful, giving my dad a hug and kissing my mother on the cheek. My arrival immediately shocked my mother out of her frustration and her rage vanished. I stuck my tongue out at her and she laughed and then stuck her tongue out at me too. All of a sudden, we were acting like children and the tension was gone. Inside, I was trying to process the immense sadness I felt but nobody knew except, perhaps, the nurse. My family home had disintegrated into a psychotic warzone and things would likely get worse before they got better.

After the nurse left, I asked the caregiver to take care of my dad while I went shopping with my mom. My mother always loved going grocery shopping and it was already Christmas Eve. We had many traditions as a family and I wasn't about to let our Christmas rituals vanish on my watch. Besides, I wanted to give my dad a break from her madness. I'm sure he needed the rest.

Growing up, we always had the same thing for dinner on Christmas Eve. It was a Swiss dish comprised of pork tenderloin and a rich cream sauce with mandarin orange segments. In earlier years, my mom would make homemade pasta to go with the sauce, but I was too afraid to give that a shot. Instead, we would have it with rice and salad. My mother and I went to the local grocery store and bought all the necessary ingredients.

There was no sight of a Christmas tree either and that was a tradition that my dad was historically in charge of. I didn't have time to get one, nor did I want to deal with that challenge with only hours left until dinner time, but we had beautiful evergreen bushes on one side of the house and I cut a few branches and tied them together to make a Christmas swag. I tied it to the back of a chair and placed it beside the fireplace.

In the end, my mom, dad and I ate our traditional Christmas Eve dinner together with a fire in the fireplace and the makeshift Christmas swag lit with Christmas lights right beside it. I even had a few gifts to put under the tree. It was beautiful in its own way. I'm proud of what I did that day. I walked into a warzone and transformed it into a civilized holiday environment in less than five hours.

> Sometimes, you have to make do with what you have. You will be confronted with imperfect situations. You will encounter obstacles. Do the best you can with what you have. It is precisely these difficult situations which test your resolve, but they also provide the opportunity for personal victories. Don't shy away from those opportunities. Embrace the challenge and demonstrate your character. Those victories, however small, will stay with you for a lifetime.

19

ORGANIZING EVENTS

I soon renamed the East Bay Entrepreneur Meetup into the Entrepreneur & Small Business Academy. We held monthly meetings that were free to attend. At the beginning, I basically featured myself as the speaker. I was determined to change my career focus into small-business marketing and this was my chance to showcase my skills. Since the podcast had done well and a number of my other tactics had also generated results, I shared my experiences and strategies with the attendees. Soon, other people wanted to speak in front of the group as well.

I learned a lot about meeting facilitation at my Toastmasters club and my Meetup members seemed to like my style. I was good at it, and our attendance grew quickly. First, we held our meetings at the Oakland library on College Avenue but it was soon too small. We then moved to the New York Life offices in Emeryville. That space accommodated about 100 people and one of their salespeople, Rodney Best, offered us the space in exchange for all the exposure to local small business owners and self-employed professionals.

The meetings continued to grow and we later moved to the Berkeley library on Kittredge Street. We could squeeze about 150 people into that space but even that became too small after a while. Finally, we ended up at the Shattuck Plaza Hotel in Berkeley, but that was about three years down the road. The point is that the group was successful, right from the start, and I was proud that I had built it myself.

I never knew that I could be a good group facilitator and it was fun to get all the attention that came with my role as organizer. This was my first brush with a celebrity-like position. Don't get me wrong. It was no big deal. But within that group, I was the leader and a lot of people started treating me really nicely. I loved the attention!

Before Christmas, I was contacted through Meetup.com by American Express. They were launching their small business OPEN program and wanted to sponsor my Entrepreneur & Small Business Academy. My group was apparently one of the 50 largest business Meetup groups in the whole country, and they wanted to invite me to New York City for the kickoff event. I couldn't reply to the email fast enough. And after a few emails back and forth, the sponsorship was confirmed and I started planning my trip to the Big Apple.

Credit Card Balance: $20,272 (January, 2008)

We all arrived in NYC in January 2008. There were three other organizers from the San Francisco Bay Area and I was thrilled to meet them all. Bill Ayers was the organizer of the San Francisco Webeneur Meetup, Edith Yeung was the organizer of the San Francisco Entrepreneur Meetup and Myles Weissleder was the organizer of the SF New Tech Meetup.

Actually, Myles wasn't able to attend the NYC trip but I had become aware of his Meetup because of the sponsorship and was impressed with what he had built. SF New Tech was the largest of the Bay Area business Meetups. Myles was a PR guy himself and launched his group to showcase bleeding-edge start-up ventures in five-minute segments. Each meeting would showcase seven startups and the founders had just five minutes to demonstrate their technology, as a bright red digital countdown clock counted down the seconds at the side of the stage.

As the clock would count down, the crowd would chant along with the digits as they came up. Ten, nine, eight, seven … it was nerve-racking for the presenters but made for an exciting and fun event for attendees. The event attracted entrepreneurs from around the world, all seeking Silicon Valley venture capital to fuel their businesses. This was a whole new world for me and I was excited to be learning more about it.

The problem with my "entrepreneur" Meetup group was that it didn't really attract entrepreneurs at all. Most of my members were self-employed service professionals and most of them were struggling financially. Of the four Meetups from the Bay Area, Bill's group and my group were comprised mostly of these struggling practitioners. Edith's group seemed to attract a higher-end audience and Myles' group was the highest on the ladder. Simply by making it essentially about raising venture capital, it immediately raised the level of people in attendance.

Very few people in my group or in Bill's group were trying to raise capital. They were just struggling to pay their monthly bills. Many of them were insurance agents, web developers, graphic designers, life coaches or multi-level marketing distributors. They were self-employed professionals, just like me. In a way, we were all a group of corporate misfits who were determined to earn a living on our own. Self-employment is a valiant pursuit but a difficult one for most. Lord knows, I was struggling to pay my own bills and there was admittedly some comfort in that shared experience in the group.

During my first few months leading the group, it became very clear to me that I needed to develop some sort of information product that I could sell to the attendees coming to my monthly events. I was also speaking at other local events but none of them paid any money, and the only way for me to earn an income by speaking was to sell something while I was there.

With the experience of my "Beyond the Rate" podcast in my back pocket, I wrote out and recorded a series of audio CDs about modern marketing. I covered all of the emerging digital-marketing channels that I was experimenting with myself. It was all very new back then, and I was desperately learning the ropes as I looked for ways to jump-start my own career.

I recorded a total of seven CDs and uploaded all the files to the Kunaki website. They had absolutely horrible customer service but their CDs were just $1.75 each with no minimums! So if I could figure out their platform, I could order just a few CDs at a time, conserving my limited funds, and then sell the mat events along the way. These sorts of options never existed before the Internet but they were now becoming increasingly common and they were the lifeline I needed to stay self-employed. I uploaded my audio files and CD cover graphics and, with my AMEX trip coming up quickly, decided to ship the first order directly to my hotel in New York City.

When I received notification that the order had arrived, I immediately went down to the lobby to pick up the package. I went back up to Bill's room and told him what I was carrying. With him sitting on a couch in his room and me sitting on the floor in front of my package, I opened those boxes and saw my own educational CDs for the first time. It was breathtaking. They looked so professional! They even had UPC barcodes on the back, just like the CDs you see in stores. This was the beginning of a new era and the two of us spoke of the upcoming income opportunities like a couple of executives negotiating billion-dollar deals.

I would later find out that I'm not actually very good at selling products (i.e., educational CDs) at the back of the room. It's a science for many and I had never done anything like it before. I did manage to sell a few of those CDs here and there and the revenue helped me pay my bills, but I lacked the confidence to make a compelling offer. In order to be an effective salesperson, you need to have complete confidence in your product, and I just wasn't there yet.

MAKE YOURSELF USEFUL

With the Sweden victory still fresh in my mind, I was more motivated than ever to get my speaking career moving. But with no notoriety to speak of, the speakers' bureaus were completely unresponsive to my inquiries. Speakers' bureaus book the majority of professional speaking business. They maintain the corporate contacts and take a commission from the speaking fee.

The speakers' bureaus never push their clients to select one speaker over another. In many cases, their clients request well-known speakers so there's no opportunity to recommend anyone anyway. In other cases, they request a particular category or topic and the bureaus respond with a grid of possible speaker options. Either way, they had no incentive to recommend me. I wasn't famous and nobody was requesting me.

When I contacted them, they asked me if I had a book or a video or ideally, both. I had neither. Maybe I could repurpose all the content from those marketing CDs and compile it into a book. Originally, those CDs started out as a second podcast series about marketing, so the CDs were already a second use of the content. Now, I thought I could compile the seven CDs into a book with seven sections.

I wrote an introduction and a conclusion, hired a friend to create a cover graphic and uploaded everything to Lulu Press. Lulu is one of the many self-publishing platforms that have emerged in recent years. It allowed me to—without asking anyone's permission or getting anyone's approval—upload my book and make it available on online bookstores like Barnes& Noble, Borders and Amazon. Today, of course, there are even more options.

After nine iterations of edits and revisions, I ended up with a beautifully printed paperback book in my hands. It was called "Make Yourself Useful: Marketing in the 21st Century." Like everything else, I immediately added it to my bio and uploaded images to my website. All of these steps were adding credibility, incrementally, to my online persona. Of course, I wasn't particularly proud of the book. It didn't flow very well and was written in a casual colloquial style, much better suited for the oral podcast format, but I didn't care. I had become an author!

A few months later, a friend helped me create a beautiful "one-sheet" about my services as a speaker, and I compiled five packages to send to five different speakers' bureaus. They included a cover letter, a copy of my book, signed of course, and my printed one-sheet for their review. I followed up with every submission and received almost nothing in return. My packages were shrugged off as being completely meaningless. They were polite, but it was clear that I would need a lot more than a book and a printed one-sheet to get their attention.

Meanwhile, I was treated differently by my audiences. The "author" label immediately put me in a different category, and the printed one-sheet was like a loaded gun. There are always people in the audience who are thinking about recommending you to other groups in which they are a member. If I had my printed one-sheets available, those people would take one and then pass it along to their contact at the other group. I can't tell you how often I got called from someone I didn't know, but who already had my printed one-sheet in their hands.

If you're building a career as a professional speaker, don't worry about the speakers' bureaus. The saying in the industry is that "you only get business from bureaus when you no longer need their help." Don't waste your time and money courting bureaus. Focus your attention on the meeting planners in the industry you're targeting. I learned quickly that books and printed one-sheets are worthless to bureaus but they both helped build my credibility with my customers and that was the bigger prize in the end.

Don't expect one marketing vehicle(like a book) or one contact (like a speakers' bureau) to catapult your business on its own. Success is rarely the result of a homerun victory. Eddie Cantor once said, "It takes 20 years to make an overnight success." The truth is that you accumulate victories along the way. I often say that, "Success is the accumulation of 10,000 tiny victories and 100,000 tiny failures." Work on building momentum and credibility, one step at a time.

Success is like constructing a building out of bricks. On its own, a brick doesn't look like much. If you saw three bricks on the side of the road, you would think they're worthless trash that someone left behind. But if you keep stacking them, one on top of the other, over and over, something starts to take shape. After a few hundred bricks, you might have a wall or two. And after a few thousand more, you might end up with an entire building.

After all that construction, you finally have something that has value. During the building process, it wasn't worth anything. It had no functionality. But after countless bricks have been diligently laid, one on top of the other, you can end up with a truly impressive structure. The same is true with success. At least that was the case with my own version of success. I never achieved anything particularly heroic or remarkable, but the accumulation of my efforts was starting to take shape.

21

EDITH YEUNG & BIZTECHDAY

Edith, the organizer of the San Francisco Entrepreneur Meetup, impressed me very much. Her group seemed much more sophisticated than mine. Actually, *she* seemed much more sophisticated than *me!* It seemed like she was playing in the big leagues while I was still playing in the sandbox.

This distinction has haunted me since the beginning and, truthfully, it still does. It's really just a distinction between cost structures. Most of the struggling self-employed professionals that attended my events, including me, were looking for free marketing channels to attract business. And to boot, the services they provided also had no real costs either. Perhaps they were consultants or graphic designers or life coaches. They did the job themselves and then billed for their time. No cost, and 100% of the billed amount represented income. That's the sandbox.

By comparison, the big leagues (which I sometimes refer to as the freeway) is where you have a cost structure in place to provide a higher-end product or service. Maybe you're paying to promote yourself. Maybe you're paying to outsource part of the service offering. Maybe you're paying to have professional office or meeting space. Whatever it is, you're providing a more sophisticated product or service offering and there are real costs involved; costs which are inevitably recouped in the selling price. These businesses havereal profit &loss statements with revenue at the top, costs of doing business in the middle and profits or losses at the bottom. Those are the big leagues.

It's always scary to jump into the big leagues. You need a viable business model and you always have to start by risking your own money. You have to take that initial chance and spend your money, not knowing if the venture will succeed or not. Looking back, I've tried to take that initial risk dozens of times. I spent my own money on different strategies but they never worked out. I tried many things but few ever succeeded enough for me to get my money back and earn a profit.

There are a lot of people around the world that are sitting around camp fires or card tables or coffee shops, brainstorming the next million-dollar business idea. Everyone has a great idea, and many fantasize how their business ideas will grow and flourish, but they don't realize that the hardest part is just getting started. People imagine step 1, step 2, step 3 and step 4. Everything makes sense. It's almost inevitable that the business will go through those steps, growing progressively bigger at each stage. What they forget is that the hardest part is just getting to step 1.

Step 1 is achieving the *proof of concept* on a viable business model. You try something. You spend money to promote an idea and it generates enough interest and enough sales that you get your initial investment back and make a profit after paying your expenses. That's step 1 and it's extremely difficult to get that far. Most things I tried never got that far. They didn't generate a profit. In fact, the vast majority resulted in an almost complete loss. I was in the sandbox.

Edith Yeung instinctively found ways of being in the big leagues. She held her meetings in beautiful hotel ballrooms. That costs money—lots of money! But her attendance was enough to pay for that expense and, presumably, leave her with a profit at the end of the night. She was holding contests and had sponsors involved who paid for their sponsorship packages and donated prizes for the contest winners. She even started a small business conference of her own. She called it BizTechDay.

Edith was a true connector. She called famous people and introduced herself without thinking twice. She did it all the time. She connected with people like Seth Godin and Tim Ferriss. She seemed to know everyone, and everyone liked Edith. She grew up in Hong Kong and had a pronounced Asian accent but that didn't hold her back at all. You can practically hear her accent in her writing. You could tell from the way she worded things that English was her second language, but it was endearing and seemed to make her even more likable.

When she launched BizTechDay, the speaker lineup was impressive and I was blown away when she asked me to be one of the emcees. She and I got along well while in New York City and she knew I was speaking regularly in the area. She also knew about my recent trip to Sweden. I told her I wanted to play a role in BizTechDay but secretly doubted she would invite me to do so. Anyway, she did and I was thrilled.

It was an intimidating opportunity. I wasn't getting paid anything, but this was a big-league event. Edith paid for hotel space and banners and food. She had a staff of people. Some were paid and others were volunteers. She advertised the event and paid some of the speakers. This was a huge financial risk but she was willing to do it. And after the whole thing was over, she made a profit. I have no idea how much but I knew she was already planning to do the event again the following year.

A year later, she did it again and it was even bigger. She was hoping for 1,000 attendees. The hotel space for a conference that big is incredibly expensive, probably in the tens of thousands of dollars. I wasn't the emcee of that second conference but I did do a couple of sessions as a speaker and was amazed at the event she put together. She didn't have 1,000 but ended up with about 850 attendees.

I spoke with Edith that morning and we talked about the stress of organizing the event. She told me that over half the attendees registered within the last 24 hours. Just one day earlier, she was expecting to lose thousands and thousands of dollars. And within a 24-hour period, over 400 people registered and paid for the event, netting her a profit in the end.

This is how the event business is going these days. People are registering later and later. It's incredibly frustrating as an event planner because you have to take such a huge financial risk and then cross your fingers that the registrations will materialize at the eleventh hour. Watching what Edith went through, I knew that I never wanted to be in the event business. It's too risky. I'd rather be the keynote speaker: more fun and less stress.

The point is that Edith was playing in the big leagues. At that point, my Meetup group was still meeting in free spaces and the events were free to attend. I quickly learned that free events attract a very different type of person than events that cost money. Even a tiny registration fee of $10 immediately weeds out the riffraff. It immediately improves the quality of people who attend. But for me, getting to that point was difficult.

Eventually, I was getting over 150 people at my monthly meetings but they were free events. Finally in 2010, I started charging $15 for my events (or $20 at the door) and my attendance immediately dropped to 40 or 50. Yes, the quality was immediately much better but I was now holding the meetings at the Shattuck Plaza Hotel and the room cost me over $400 to rent and they wanted to increase the rate. At that point, I was indeed in the big leagues but just barely getting by.

This whole experience dramatically increased the amount of respect I had for real entrepreneurs who had developed sustainable business models. Few people realize how difficult that is, but my experience with Meetup made it crystal clear. It's easy to fantasize about step 1, step 2 and step 3, but the hardest part is getting to step 1. Getting that far is the true victory. Growing the venture after the proof of concept is in place? That's the easy part.

BAD SPEECH TITLES

It was February, 2008, and I decided to start speaking as much as I could, regardless if they paid me or not. I heard that local community organizations like the Rotary Club, Kiwanis Club and Lions Club were looking for speakers on a regular basis. I also become aware of an exploding number of local Meetup groups and they were looking for speakers as well.

Credit Card Balance: $23,309 (March, 2008)

I did some research in March and discovered the club locator on the Rotary Club's main website. By entering a ZIP code, you could immediately get a listing of local clubs along with their current club presidents and contact information. I compiled a list of every single Rotary Club in the San Francisco Bay Area and also Sacramento. There were over 150 clubs! They were everywhere and I had never even realized it. It reminded me of Toastmasters. There too, there were clubs everywhere that I had never been aware of before.

I started contacting the club presidents. Within three or four calls, it became clear that I needed a PDF proposal that I could email to them for consideration. I called my program "Driving Internet Traffic" and created a nicely formatted one-page PDF file describing the program. It was modeled on my printed one-sheet and included a photo of me along with my expanding bio. It looked good and I was excited to get their response. As usual, it was a disappointment.

The Rotary Club sees itself as a community organization and a number of the people I contacted said my program was too business-oriented for their guidelines. That was silly in my opinion, because these clubs are generally seen as business networking groups by their members. Most of the members are there to meet other local business professionals, but that didn't seem to matter. If I wanted to speak at their local meetings, I would need a program that was more community-oriented.

This was early 2008 and the Obama presidential campaign was in full swing. He was leveraging all the new social networking sites and generating a huge amount of excitement among younger voters. Meanwhile, these Rotary Clubs were attracting no younger members at all. Many of the members were near retirement age and the clubs were all struggling to attract new, younger members.

I decided to create a program that featured all these new social networking platforms and position them as communication channels to engage new younger tech-savvy members. But in my haste, I ended up writing the absolute worst possible title imaginable. Even worse, I didn't realize how bad it was for a full year. For some reason, it just never crossed my mind that my program title was offensive and controversial, particularly when considering the average demographic of Rotary Club members.

My program was called "Touching a Younger Audience."

It was awful. Embarrassing. I had learned the importance of a good title from my experience in Sweden but for some reason, the lesson fell on deaf ears and I plowed forward with the inappropriate title. Nevertheless, it met the community guidelines and therefore achieved the objective. After creating a PDF one-sheet, I started contacting clubs again and received a more favorable response.

This all happened over just two days and by the end of the second day, I had contacted 47 different Rotary Clubs. And although it took some time for the back-and-forth to unfold, those initial inquiries eventually resulted in 27 speaking engagements. I had Rotary Clubs booked out as far as the eye could see. None of them paid me anything but it was still very exciting. I sold a few CDs and the exposure would undoubtedly push me in the right direction.

The interesting thing is that I began to really like the "Touching a Younger Audience" program. At the beginning, I much preferred the "Driving Internet Traffic" program but I rarely got a chance to deliver it, so all my experience was with the newer program. And almost daily, I would incorporate new information, new case histories I discovered online and new slides to explain my perspective on the burgeoning social Internet. Barack Obama's election campaign was taking America by storm and my program became more dynamic and relevant by the day.

Eventually, someone's facial expression when I mentioned the title was enough for it to finally sink in. It never crossed my mind that my title was alluding to pedophilia. I should've called it "Reaching a Younger Audience" or "Engaging Tomorrow's Members" or something like that. Anyway, I didn't, but finally understood all the strange comments and chuckling I had encountered on my travels.

By this time, the term *social media* was becoming the most common term for all things online and social. After some brainstorming, I renamed the program "Social Media Victories: Real Businesses, Real Campaigns, Real Results." The improvement was dramatic and immediate, and I was way ahead of the curve.

SOCIAL MEDIA VICTORIES

The social media topic was hot and everyone wanted to talk about it. The older Baby Boom generation was caught off guard at first and felt vulnerable to the new communication channels evolving all around them. Stories began to emerge of young Millennials stealing business from established professionals who had spent their whole lives marketing with direct mail and print advertising. All of the professional associations needed social media speakers and I had a great program. It was so good, in fact, that it took me all around the world.

My program was good for a number of reasons, none of which I truly appreciated at the time. I just assumed that all of my programs would be received by audiences the same way. Not so. This program was special. It had fascinating case histories. Some were funny and entertaining. Others were innovative and insightful. They were all shocking and amazing given the newness of the medium. And it ended with a poignant and thought-provoking conclusion.

Think back 20 years or even 100 years ago. It's always been the same. People have always looked at the *source* of information first and then the information itself, or the *content,* second. In other words, they wanted to know where the information was coming from before they evaluated the information itself. If it was on the evening news, it must be important. If it was written in the *Wall*

Street Journal, it must be true. If he or she went to Harvard, it must be correct.

Today, that has completely turned around. Today, people see the information—the content—before they know where it came from. At one time or another, we've all had an image or a video pop up on our Facebook timeline and watched it before we knew who created it. In those cases, we saw the content before we knew the source. It's the exact opposite of the previous model. This is a wholesale shift in the way we consume content, and it's ushering in a whole new world of opportunity for regular people like you and me: opportunities that never existed before.

All of the old-fashioned assumptions have disappeared. They don't mean anything anymore. Oh, so you went to Harvard? Who cares? So you have 18 years' experience? Who cares? It's not that those things don't matter anymore. They do matter, but they matter less than they used to. Before the social media revolution, content needed to come from credible sources to attract the masses. Today, anyone who produces compelling content can attract a global audience within a few hours.

In the old world, you needed "third-party institutional credibility" to build an audience. You needed a degree from an Ivy League school. You needed a decade's experience with an industry-leading company. Your book had to be published by a national publisher. You had to accomplish something truly incredible and have it verified by an established organization. Today, that's no longer true. If you have good content, the world is your oyster. For a guy like me, with no traditional credentials to speak of, it was a dream come true.

The Internet allows anyone to create and share content in the public domain. And because people are using social media platforms to discover and share content within their peer groups, good quality content can get shared and passed along in short order. So if you're creating good quality content, even if you're completely unknown at the beginning, you can build an audience and enjoy the same credibility as someone with twice the money and three times the education.

This is exactly what happened to me: I was a living, breathing example of the social media revolution myself. During my presentation, I could make references to my own journey and the things I was doing to advance my own career. It was all consistent with the other case histories I was presenting. There was perfect congruence between the message and the messenger. I had no traditional credentials myself, yet I was there as the featured speaker.

My Social Media Victories program was strong. It made people think and every time I delivered it, people came up and told me that I *had* to deliver the same program to some other group that they belonged to. The referral potency was amazing and I began to realize the importance of "the problem" in a successful keynote speaking program.

> The most effective keynote topics are those that address the biggest problems. That's what drives relevance. If the keynote addresses a major problem, the content is more relevant for attendees, and relevance is the single best measure of success for a keynote speech. What's the problem with *your* keynote addresses? What is *your* target market struggling with?

Social Media Victories ended up taking me to dozens of events across the country as well as events in Canada, Mexico, Aruba, the Cayman Islands, Stockholm (again), Helsinki, Lisbon, New Delhi, Jaipur and Bangkok. It was an amazing run and I thought I was finally out of the woods. I thought I had made it but yet again, I would soon be proven wrong by the changing currents of life.

BUILDING AN EMAIL LIST

E veryone who was advancing in the field of Internet marketing was building massive email lists. People like John Reese, Andy Jenkins and Frank Kern were offering free reports and helpful information in exchange for email addresses and I needed to do the same thing. I created a 52-week course where subscribers got one email each week for a full year. Each email contained a marketing tip along with a checklist to put the tip into action.

Over the course of two or three days, I wrote a full outline with all the tips listed and a few bullet points on each one. Outlines are incredibly useful because you can easily reorder topics and move stuff around. Just by starting the process of writing down your thoughts, you inevitably get a flood of other ideas which you add under the appropriate topic or subtopic, and the outline quickly takes shape.

Many people instinctively believe that I wrote all of the 52 weekly tips by the time I launched the program, but nothing could be further from the truth. I wrote the first two tips and then created the sign-up form on my website and signed up myself. That made me the very first subscriber. From that point on, I only needed to stay ahead of myself to ensure the program would be seamless for everyone who subscribed thereafter. As long as I wrote and uploaded one new tip each week, it would all appear pre-written by future subscribers.

This ended up being a great way to force myself into a consistent content-generation schedule. With a detailed outline to refer back to, I could write four or five emails in one sitting and upload them all to my email auto responder and then relax for a month until I started to run out again. For those who don't know, an email auto responder is a platform that manages these automated email distribution programs and includes unsubscribe links at the bottom of each email, as well as tools to manage the subscriber list.

Credit Card Balance: $22,765 (February, 2008)

I launched my email course in February 2008, and filled in the additional email tips as the weeks and months went by. As usual, the program subscriptions fell far short of my initial hopes. At its height, I had about 1,000 people on the list. That's not bad but it's also far too few to leverage with other affiliate-type marketing opportunities. A 1% conversion rate, for example, would yield just 10 buyers, so the program never contributed anything to my revenue, but it did lead to plenty of other benefits.

My marketing tips were good. I knew a lot about the new Internet marketing platforms and had a no-nonsense approach when explaining them. People sometimes replied to those emails and thanked me for the advice or told me about their own experiences. Eventually, a few people suggested that I compile these tips into a book. Another book? I had never considered that option and was reminded how my first book was nothing more than the written text from my marketing podcast, which had already been repurposed into my educational CDs. The same written content had become three distinctly different products and it looked like that pattern might repeat itself here.

This idea started to take shape during the fall months of 2008. I had only written the first 36 tips at that point, but the idea of writing a second book captured my imagination. I learned a lot with my first book and believed I could do better the second time around. Besides, I was kind of embarrassed by my first book and always felt self-conscious when people bought it. Meanwhile, I was proud of my marketing tips and would have been happy to have them available for sale as a book one day.

GETTING NERVOUS

I ended up speaking at 71 different events in 2008 and 127 in 2009. I spoke everywhere: Rotary Clubs, Meetup groups, networking events and church basements. And to be clear, of the 71 events I spoke at in 2008, I only got paid for two of them and only traveled for one. In 2009, I got paid for six events and traveled for five. That means I did 69 free events in 2008 and 121 free events in 2009.

My gross revenue in 2008 was just $27,000 and it rose slightly to $36,000 in 2009, and that's *before* my expense deductions! My financial struggle was still in full swing and my freezer was still full of chicken thighs. Most of the social-media referral magic didn't translate into paid gigs until 2010 and even then, the results weren't glorious. It would eventually take until 2013 for me to finally pay off all my credit cards and personal debts.

The point is that I was speaking all the time. I once spoke at three different events in a single day. And during all those events, I slowly got used to the jitters I felt every time I stood up in front of a group of people. My ability to channel my nervous energy depended on the audience and little circumstantial details that were beyond my own control. The biggest problem was the dichotomy between my assumed status as the speaker and the financial reality in my life.

The contradiction was visceral for me. It was perpetually etched in my mind and if the audience consisted of successful established people, I feltparalyzed. Even though I knew my topic, I had no right to educate these people on anything. They were probably all making a lot more money than me. They probably owned homes, had spouses and, in most cases, had growing families as well. I had none of those things and was constantly afraid that I would somehow get found out.

Credit Card Balance: $26,277 (June, 2008)

One Saturday morning, I spoke at the Breakfast Blogging Club, which was a group of mostly women who got together monthly to work on their respective blogs in each other's company. It was started by a member of my Entrepreneur & Small Business Academy and she invited me to speak for her members. Since it was on a Saturday morning, I felt like I should dress more casually than I did for other events. I wore a blue button-down shirt, untucked, with some nice jeans. That was a mistake.

It happened before I even stood up to speak. The energy in the room was different than I was used to and I immediately felt apprehensive. That nervous feeling often goes away after a few minutes but in this case, it resulted in armpit sweat and the moisture changed the color of my shirt from a light blue to a very dark blue. It was the fabric. I had no idea that would happen. But I noticed it and that, of course, dramatically amplified the problem.

My breaths got shallower and shallower. My rib cage felt like it was about to snap with tension. The sweat seemed to pour from my armpits and the stains grew and grew. I kept my arms close to my sides to try and hide what was happening but it was impossible to hide entirely and I could see the women glancing down at my shirt instead of at my face. It was horrible and nothing could slow it down. By the end of my presentation, my shirt was completely wet down to my waist on both sides.

It was awkward at the end. Everybody knew I was falling apart. Everyone knew there was a problem. Within 10 seconds of finishing, I excused myself and walked outside of the building. It was cool outside and you could see steam coming out from my shirt. The sweat soaked right into my jeans and my underwear on either side. I was humiliated.

Eventually, I went back into the café where the event was being held. By now, the women were chatting with each other and working on their laptops. The focus was no longer on me and I immediately felt more comfortable. A couple of them asked me questions and I was able to answer them calmly. The questions also allowed me to showcase some of my expertise and most of the other women listened as well. The dialog continued and I was able to vindicate myself somewhat before leaving about an hour later. That was a gift.

I learned something that day. I learned the value of wearing a blazer. No kidding. You might be surprised to know the real reasons why people do what they do. The answers might sometimes surprise you. In my case, I vowed to never again begin a presentation without a blazer on. I could always take it off during the presentation but I would always start by wearing it. That way, if the jitters consumed me again, nobody would know.

A good friend struggles with this as well and like me, he is also in the public eye regularly. He literally has ice packs that he stuffs into his shirt before stressful events. It's his way of managing the situation. We are all human beings and we all struggle with different issues. The trick is to be real and candid with yourself and take the steps you need to take to keep things humming along. I found my own solutions and you will undoubtedly do the same.

Visit **Keynote**Mastery.com to download worksheet #4 on taking action.

26

CHRISTMAS, 2008

Credit Card Balance: $20,425 (December, 2008)

Christmas was approaching and it was again my turn to visit my parents in Vancouver. I'm the youngest of four kids and we all committed to visiting once each year. That way, my parents would have visitors once every three months. Ever since the meltdown in 2007, these visits weren't much fun anymore. My mother was getting worse and worse and my dad was basically in denial about her situation and, truthfully, about his own as well.

The previous May, things came to a head. While having some guests over for an afternoon tea, my dad was trying to move from his wheelchair to one of the dining room chairs and let his weight fall back too quickly. He hit the chair and then the two of them— the chair and his body on top of it—fell backward and his head crashed through the full-length glass pane on the patio door. He ended up with cuts on his head, with pieces of glass stuck under the skin, and my mother immediately panicked and defiantly re- fused to call for medical help.

Eventually after some period of protest and wrangling from their guests, an ambulance was called and my dad received stitches at the hospital. But it had become clear that things weren't safe anymore. We siblings were all very frustrated with my mother's behavior and my father's refusal to acknowledge her failings. My mother was the center of his world and he protected her to the end, even when his own safety was at risk.

Much later, I heard about another episode when he was sitting in his wheelchair in the den (his office) and didn't have the strength to move the chair. Since his month-long stay in the hospital in 2007, he had become increasingly weak and fragile. Anyway, mom went on another one of her rampages and he could hear her crashing around the house but could do nothing about it. He was unable to move the wheelchair and sat there, helpless, as she yelled and screamed around the house, not even knowing herself what she was doing.

It's quite common for dementia to get worse at night. They call it "sundown syndrome," and my mother has a classic case. Things get crazy at night. All my life, she had trouble sleeping but in her later years, things got a lot more intense. And of course, my dad saw it as his responsibility to keep her calm, so he would stay up with her until she calmed down. Sometimes, that didn't happen until 5:00 or 6:00 in the morning.

We heard about this pattern from the caregivers. They would tell us that my parents had been up all night long. My mother would finally fall asleep when the darkness subsided and my dad would be left to fend for himself, at least until the caregivers came back upstairs in the morning. Many times, he would end up sleeping in his wheelchair.

Once evening arrived, mom demanded that the caregivers go downstairs where the other bedrooms were. Growing up, all four of us kids slept in bedrooms downstairs and my parents had the one remaining bedroom on the main floor. Anyway, my mother would scream at the caregivers if they came upstairs so they tried to stay down there unless absolutely necessary.

My poor dad was completely exhausted most of the time. He was never able to get a good night's sleep. The thing that bothered me the most was that he never stuck up for himself. He never expressed his own needs. His only concern was my mother, and so much of her behavior was cruel and selfish. Yes, I know much of it was a function of her mental illness but we had already seen early signs of this behavior while we were growing up—my dad always stuck up for her no matter what.

Anyway, that particular night was no exception and my dad was left in his wheelchair all night, facing the bookshelf, completely helpless while my mom tore the house apart. Nobody came to get him. Of course, he had no way of getting to the restroom or getting any food or water. He probably got a little bit of sleep while sitting there, but his feeling of helplessness was what hurt me the most. My father hated feeling helpless. He was a doer. He got stuff done. And for him to have to sit there, hearing my mother in other parts of the house, knowing she had long ago forgotten that her husband was stranded in the den, it must have been horrible.

My mother no longer knew he was her husband anyway. She now believed he was actually her own father and that some evil actors had stolen her husband from her. Of course, the most likely culprit was my dad, her father, so she would regularly scream at him and demand that he return her husband to her. Meanwhile, he was sitting right there! My dad was 100% devoted to my mom and had to endure such hurtful, horrible things. I can't imagine the pain he felt inside.

We had been coordinating closely with the community service organization that was responsible for my parents' neighborhood. It's called Pacific Spirit Health and is funded by the provincial government. They knew the situation with my parents and we had discussed the eventual transition to a seniors' facility for some months already. There was no way my parents would ever leave the house voluntarily so we reported all of these incidents to build a file that would eventually justify taking them out by force. I know that sounds awful, but the situation was completely dysfunctional. They weren't getting any sleep and my father was living in a highly unsafe environment.

The decision was finally made in May, 2008, and we had a chance to warn my dad over the phone before it happened. "They're gonna take you guys out of there on Saturday, dad. Do you understand that?" He hated the situation and cried on cue but also understood that it was inevitable. Just two days later, they took them to a locked hospital ward where my mother was, for the first time, forced to take medication. My sister and I arrived approximately one week later.

My mother had always refused to take medication. It's really too bad because she would've benefited from it more than most. When she was given medication before, she defiantly flushed it down the toilet. The people at Pacific Spirit Health told us that this transition would happen only once. The first time, my mother would be administered medication without requesting her consent but after that, she would immediately be more calm and manageable and would likely accept it without resistance in the future.

The project for my sister and I was to get them completely moved in to the seniors' facility after a one-month stay in the hospital ward. It was a huge job and one I will remember for the rest of my life. But in the end, we did manage to get them into one of the nicest nursing homes in Vancouver and furnished their apartment with many of their favorite pieces from the house. It was sad and it was difficult, but it got done and I'm proud of that move. Anyway, this would be the first Christmas in the nursing home and I was hoping it would be a significant improvement from the Christmas one year earlier.

The snow was already falling when I arrived. Situated on the west coast, it doesn't snow very often in Vancouver. The climate is similar to Seattle. But this year, it was cold outside and they were projecting significant accumulations over the coming days. I was staying at a friend's place, but it was being renovated and only had plywood with no insulation for one wall. Andrew said he didn't want to turn the heat on because it would all leak out through that one wall. I would have to make do, with snow falling outside and no heat inside. Bad start! The good news was that he would be staying at his girlfriend's apartment so I had his place all to myself.

The snow came down like crazy that year. It definitely looked like Christmas: the streets were covered in snow and on one evening, the bus couldn't even get up the hill at 33rd Avenue, leaving me to walk the last ten blocks in the snow. Vancouver is notoriously ill equipped to handle snow. Andrew's place was freezing and had no Internet connection. There was ice in the kitchen sink each morning. It seemed like everything was lining up to make this a difficult visit.

My parents were doing poorly. My dad, in particular, had aged significantly and was now having his food cut up into pieces to help him swallow. He had lost his ability to clear his throat properly so all of his nasal cavities were filled with phlegm and nothing was getting down. Sometimes he would manage to cough some phlegm up in the afternoon and the blue pills from that morning were still sitting there, undigested from hours earlier. My dad was dying and I could do nothing about it.

One morning, I decided to keep most of the day for myself and only visit my parents for dinner. During the day, I camped out in the coffee shop across the street from Andrew's place and worked on my marketing tips. I was determined to finish the series and had also committed to turning it into my second book. That meant I had to write an introduction and a conclusion and also edit all the individual tips to avoid references to the email course. There was much work to do and I set up my laptop at a corner table and started typing away, snow still falling outside.

It seemed almost impossible for me to focus on the task at hand. My father's hopeless situation was racing through my mind. At the same time, I was harboring intense anger against my mom. She was making everything worse and there was no way of stopping her because she literally didn't know what she was doing. I started to feel that now-familiar pressure build up in my throat and before I could get my emotions in check, tears started streaming down my cheeks and I sat there, sobbing.

Life isn't perfect. There are plenty of circumstances that will try to derail you from pursuing your dreams. At some point, you have to take personal responsibility for your life and commit to those dreams, regardless of the obstacles you encounter. The only person who's going to improve your situation is you. Embrace the obstacles as part of the journey. As soon as they happen, they become part of your path. They become part of your story. And in the end, they become part of your personal victory as well.

I did get a little bit of work done that day, but the time I spent with my parents was frustrating and my personal life didn't seem much better. I was still struggling financially and was still single as well. It felt like an endless battle with very few rewards. I needed a break. I needed something to go my way.

WEBIFY YOUR BUSINESS

Credit Card Balance: $25,525 (February, 2009)

I finished all 52 marketing tips for my email course by February 2009, and added eight more for my book. The introduction and conclusion were done and I was ready to go to print. But what should I call it?

During the Toastmasters speaking contest the previous year, I had met a pretty Romanian woman whom I dated for a short time. The relationship never amounted to anything, but I liked her and was fascinated with the work she was doing. She was smart and was in charge of the e-learning department at AT&T, but she left that job to become self-employed, just like me. Like Edith Yeung and her San Francisco Entrepreneur Meetup, this woman was ready to play in the big leagues.

Her name was Carmen. She teamed up with a professional colleague and they started a training company called Rexi Media. The company taught professionals how to give more effective presentations and she was in the process of writing a book on the same topic. When we first met, it seemed like we had so much in common. I was hopeful that the relationship would develop but the spark was never there and it soon fizzled out.

It was impossible for me not to periodically visit the Rexi Media website. I was still somewhat smitten and was simultaneously fascinated by the company's quick ascent into an established training organization. One day, I clicked on their testimonials page and watched a couple of videos of their past clients raving about the training they had received. One guy said that they had helped him "rexify" his presentations. Rexify. Wow. They had established their own corporate lexicon!

My book was comprised of 60 short marketing tips, almost all of them pertaining to new and innovative online marketing strategies. It was best tailored to small business owners or self-employed professionals who were trying to market their products or services online. Essentially, the book would help them bring their businesses onto the web, and that's when it struck me. With thoughts of Carmen drifting through my mind, I decided on the title *Webify Your Business: Internet Marketing Secrets for the Self-Employed*.

The "webify" brand would end up following me around for over two years. It had a nice ring to it and was easily understood when people first heard it. After a handful of iterations and revisions, I received my first order in early April 2009, only a week before I received the phone call.

Credit Card Balance: $26,245 (April, 2009)

The call was from my parents' doctor. My dad had been struggling with a cough and the doctor had come to visit. He did a few tests and determined that it was nothing serious, but the cough didn't get better. It got worse and my dad was eventually taken to the hospital. After more tests, it turned out that he had developed pneumonia.

People with Parkinson's almost never die of the disease. Instead, they eventually lose control of their ability to swallow and the phlegm that builds up in their nasal cavities starts draining into their lungs instead of their stomach. Once that process begins, it's difficult to stop and infections soon follow. That's what pneumonia is and that's how most Parkinson's patients die. We all knew this was coming but I was surprised at how quickly it had snuck up on us. A week earlier, everything was somewhat normal but now, things were suddenly critical.

I asked how serious the situation was and the doctor told me that this was the time to fly in. He said this would be the end. When I arrived in Vancouver, my dad was still somewhat conscious: not really, but somewhat. He had an oxygen mask on but could still respond by opening his eyes and whispering a few words. His blood pressure was 39 over 18. The doctor said that the elevated oxygen intake was damaging his brain and that if he survived, he would never be the same. He would be left with brain damage.

I sat with my dad and put a copy of *Webify Your Business* in his hands. I told him it was my second book and that I was much more proud of this one than the first one I had showed him a year earlier. It was selfish to trumpet my own book during his last hours but it was important to me, and I really wanted him to know that I was making some progress in my career, despite the dismal outward appearances. His eyes opened slightly and he saw the book in his hands. He smiled briefly and then started to cry. I cried too.

Growing up, my dad had a dream for a better life, and he achieved it for himself. He married my mother, a cultured European woman, and built a respectable life for himself and his family. He chased his dream, just as I was chasing mine, and his dream had come true. Whether he realized it or not, he was my inspiration through the struggles. I didn't even realize it myself at that time, but I realize it now. He was the model I followed. He gave me an example to live up to. He was my quiet hero.

Who inspires you? Think about it. I never realized how much my dad inspired me until he was already gone. Don't let that happen to you. We all have people in our lives who we emulate and learn from. Sometimes we're not even aware of it. Figure out who those people are in your life. Take a more deliberate approach to that learning process. Give them an opportunity to teach you. It might be more rewarding for them than it is for you.

My brother and sister had flown in and one of the caregivers was with us as well. The challenge was to keep my mom distracted and calm. She always appeared lucid in situations like this but we all knew she had very little idea what was happening. The doctors pulled me aside and gave me the prognosis and it was obviously bleak. "What would you like to do?" they asked. "Let him go," I said. We all agreed. Even my mother, once told of the situation, immediately agreed as if she understood the situation.

The doctors removed the oxygen mask and my dad's breaths became weak and shallow. He didn't seem uncomfortable, just fading out. A few more minutes passed and he took his last breath. I was holding his right arm and my mother was holding his right hand. My sister was holding his left arm and my brother was holding his left leg. And Ben, one of the incredible caregivers that had worked with our parents for the past two years, was holding his right leg.

My dad's funeral was on May 2nd, 2009, and my siblings agreed to let me deliver the eulogy. For that, I am eternally grateful. You can read it here:

http://www.keynotemastery.com/eulogy/

SWEDEN IN THE SUMMER

2009 was the year when I spoke 147 times. I was speaking everywhere and Lennart Svanberg from Sweden had invited me to speak again at that year's conference. It was being held in Stockholm at the end of May so I got back into my speaking focus soon after my dad's funeral.

Credit Card Balance: $27,442 (May, 2009)

It was interesting to see Stockholm less than a month before the summer solstice. My first trip there was just three weeks before the winter solstice and there was a huge difference between the two. This time, the sun started to come up at about 3:45 AM and didn't go down until almost 10:00 PM. It was bright and sunny all the time.

Lennart paid for my hotel reservations this time and also agreed to pay me a percentage of the revenue from a full-day seminar that I would give on the second day of the conference. My keynote was on the first day. If it went well, more people would register for my full-day workshop, he would make more money and I would make more as well. I had an incentive to perform.

The hotels in Europe are very different from the hotels we have here in North America. The beds are small and the bathrooms are even smaller. Everything seems very utilitarian. My room was actually two floors *down* from the hotel lobby. Yes, that means it was in the basement and had no windows. In fact, it didn't even have a bathroom and the only way to activate the electricity was to put your room key into a slot in the wall.

That wasn't a problem until I had to pee in the middle of the night. In order to access the shared bathroom down the hall, I had to remove my room key from the wall slot which immediately reset my clock. When I got back to my room, I had no idea what time it was and hadn't turned my cell phone on for fear of massive roaming charges. I had to go upstairs to the lobby and ask for the time and then go back down to reset my clock and alarm. Getting back to sleep after that was impossible.

I hate to say it, but like my mom, my anxiety emerges at night. It's sometimes hard for me to sleep. At that point, I had never slept on a plane, at least not for more than an hour or so, and sleeping before important events was also unlikely. Meanwhile, the pressure for me to perform in Sweden was significant and I lay in bed, peaceful but awake, for the next three hours before it was time to get up.

My keynote went well and almost 20 people signed up for my full-day workshop. Lennart was happy and I was terrified. My speaking style works really well with large audiences but I always struggle with small ones. Also, I've never been good at facilitating workshop-style events. I'm better at hour-long keynote programs.

I had only slept for about three hours the first night and didn't sleep at all on the second. Yet again, I was peaceful. I did indeed get some rest, but I never actually fell asleep. I had over 300 PowerPoint slides for the next day and my mind was spinning with all the details. When it was finally time to get up again, I was running exclusively on adrenaline.

The day went reasonably well, but my content wasn't a good fit for the audience. The people in attendance were corporate employees. They worked for large corporations and needed corporate solutions to the evolving social media landscape. My suggestions were guerrilla tactics. They were essentially tips and tricks that small businesses and self-employed professionals could use to get exposure for free. They were tactics designed for my own situation and none of these people were in my situation.

The mismatch was clear, but I think the attendees appreciated the passion I brought to the topic. They soon understood my angle and while it didn't solve all of their problems, they definitely saw how industry newcomers could subvert their stodgy corporate marketing campaigns on the emerging social media platforms. In the end, they left smiling, Lennart made a solid profit and I got paid. I slept for 12 hours that night.

PLATFORM SPEAKING VS. KEYNOTE SPEAKING

There's a huge distinction in the speaking business between "platform speakers" and "keynote speakers." Platform speakers are always selling stuff. It might be a DVD set. It might be an expensive workshop or coaching program. It might even be consulting services. By contrast, keynote speakers are paid a fixed fee to speak at an event and aren't selling anything except their message. In fact, if they tried to sell something, they would never be hired back.

The vast majority of speakers (possibly as many as 90%) are actually platform speakers. They almost never get paid a speaking fee and instead earn their income from product or program sales. They also generally have to promote their own events, so it's always a game of getting registrations and putting butts in seats. They offer discounts if you buy today and learn sophisticated techniques to "sell from the platform."

Platform speakers also speak at other people's events. In those situations, they would not be responsible for driving registrations but would pay the organizer a percentage of their sales revenue. This revenue split compensates the event organizer for taking the financial risk and promoting the event. For platform speakers, the size and quality of the audience is of prime importance.

"The Real Estate Wealth Expo" and "The Money Show" are both great examples of large platform-speaking events. They attract tens of thousands of attendees and then get platform speakers to sell their programs, earning a percentage of the revenue in the process. They also pay a few famous speakers to headline the event because those names help drive registration for the event as a whole. If they can amass a good audience, platform speakers will sell more products and they'll make more as well.

The speakers who speak at the Real Estate Wealth Expo (which featured Donald Trump in years past) actually *pay* $50,000 plus 50% of their sales revenue to get a time slot on the main stage, but some of them gross over $400,000 in sales during their 90-minute sessions. In that scenario, they would give the organizers $200,000 (50% of revenue) plus $50,000 (or $250,000 in total) and then net $150,000 for 90 minutes' work. Meanwhile, the organizers use the $250,000 to pay for the facility and all the marketing, and hopefully have a profit left over at the end. It's big business.

When people think about professional speakers, they often think about people like Tony Robbins, T. Harv Eker, Suze Orman or Robert Kiyosaki. These are all platform speakers. Yes, they may get keynote speaking opportunities from time to time, but they earn most of their revenue by selling their own products and programs. It's worth noting that the income potential of platform speakers is much higher than for keynote speakers. The most successful non-celebrity keynote speakers earn about $600,000 or $700,000 per year. The most successful platform speakers earn millions.

Just to clarify, there are indeed keynote speakers who earn more than $700,000. I once spoke at an event for United Healthcare where Condoleezza Rice also spoke. I got paid $6,000 and she got paid $150,000. When Donald Trump spoke at the Real Estate Wealth Expo, he was the headline speaker and charged one million dollars for each of six events in six different cities. Bill Clinton earned $104,900,000 for 542 events between 2001 and 2013. That's an average of $193,000 for each one!

These people can charge that much because they're celebrities and their participation drives registrations for the event organizers. That's not true for most keynote speakers. Non-celebrity speakers might have significant followings and accumulate some notoriety along the way, but their participation doesn't affect registrations significantly. So for normal keynote speakers, $700,000 is an upper limit to earnings.

It's also worth noting that there's no barrier to entry for platform speakers. Anyone can start promoting their own events and try to sell stuff to the people who attend. As a result, the quality level, on average, is lower for platform speakers. Of course, the best ones are incredible. Tony Robbins is an amazing speaker, but there is also a ton of local people flogging their own programs and the quality level is lower for them.

By contrast, keynote speaking has huge barriers to entry. Someone has to hire you. Corporations have thousands of speakers to choose from and they'll pick the very best speaker they can find within their budget. Also, speakers' bureaus have no interest in promoting newbie speakers who are not yet established. They generally focus on well-known speakers who are requested by their corporate clients. As a result of these barriers to entry, the quality level of keynote speakers is generally much higher.

Very few speakers are keynote speakers and that's one of the reasons it's such an alluring career. I've never met a platform speaker who didn't fantasize about getting keynote speaking engagements. As a keynote speaker, you're not responsible for promoting the event and your income isn't tied to your sales numbers. You're paid to show up, deliver your message and leave. That's it.

The good news is that there's a *ton* of business in the keynote-speaking category. On any given week day in a metropolitan city like San Francisco, there are probably dozens of people who are paid to speak. Every downtown hotel is hosting business groups and many of them have at least one paid speaker on the agenda. Meanwhile, there are countless other events taking place in museums, schools, universities, churches and of course, conference and convention centers. There's definitely no shortage of speaking opportunities.

Visit **Keynote**Mastery.com to download worksheet #5 on the differences between platform speakers and keynote speakers.

JEFF & KANE

J eff & Kane contacted me in January 2009. They were a duo and wanted to speak at the Entrepreneur & Small Business Academy. There were many people who contacted me about speaking for the group, so I usually met their introductions with skepticism, but I was impressed with Jeff on the phone and intrigued with their "Unfair Sales Magic" presentation title. It was a great title! I added them to the calendar for our February meeting.

Credit Card Balance: $25,525 (February, 2009)

We had at least 100 people at that meeting and Jeff & Kane set up tall director's chairs at the front of the room. They didn't speak like other speakers. They introduced and discussed a particular subject for a few minutes and then engaged the audience with questions and exercises. They were good at it. They even invited a couple of people to come up to the front, and they then worked with those individuals right in front of the audience. My members loved it.

Throughout their presentation, they referred to the work they did for clients and the improvements those people experienced, not only in their businesses but also in their personal lives. At the end, they casually mentioned that they had a three-day intensive weekend workshop coming up and if anyone from my group wanted to come, they would only charge $99 for the whole weekend. At least a dozen people lined up to register.

I later heard that this weekend event was a huge success, and everyone I knew who attended was impressed with the program. Apparently, they also had a whole series of other more advanced three-day weekend programs that they sold during the initial weekend event. These more advanced programs were much more expensive—like, in the thousands of dollars —but some of my members purchased those as well.

During the years that followed, I got to know these two guys very well. I spoke at their events on many occasions, even though I generally didn't sell anything, and got a firsthand look at their growing business. They had it down to a science. They had expensive training programs available and knew exactly what their average revenue-per-attendee had to be. They were making huge money, all while I was still struggling to pay my bills.

On the other hand, I had a natural disdain for the sales process they were creating. I knew one lady who liquidated her IRA in order to take one of their expensive weekend workshops. I knew her well and was certain she could never become the "industry rockstar" the workshop promised. In the end, I knew she was wasting her money.

It's not that Jeff and Kane were doing anything wrong. They weren't, and their programs were full of awesome tactical advice for savvy business owners. That wasn't the problem. The problem was that this particular lady was a quiet and somewhat shy ex-accountant who was now self-employed as a result of being laid off. There was no way she would transform herself into the business dynamo that leveraged all of Jeff and Kane's strategies.

There were dozens of examples like this. It seemed like the people least able to achieve the desired results were the first ones to buy the programs. Because they weren't natural winners to begin with, they could least afford it. These were people who were struggling and here they were, liquidating IRAs in some cases, to chase their dreams. I certainly didn't want those unrealistic hopes and dreams on my shoulders. It would be difficult for me to sell programs the way they did.

At some point along the way, I decided that I much preferred selling to corporations over selling to individuals. Once the invoice went to a corporation, I had no guilt anymore. They had the money. They had budgets for this sort of thing. The money they paid me would never leave them destitute or bankrupt. It was part of the marketing budget and if I ever got that type of business, I didn't expect to feel uncomfortable about it at all. It would take another two years before I'd get to test that hypothesis.

Anyway, their approach was obviously platform speaking. I didn't pay them anything to speak to my Meetup group but they sold registrations to their weekend event and left that evening with at least $1,200 more than they came with. Then, at the workshop itself, they sold more advanced programs and made more money as a result. The whole revenue model was based on selling programs from the stage.

Jeff & Kane were platform speakers, and they were good at it. Their questions and exercises were all designed to increase sales, and they worked like a charm. Jeff & Kane were both Neuro-linguistic Programming (NLP) master practitioners. NLP is the study of linguistic patterns and how they can be used to affect human behavior. Basically, the way Jeff & Kane spoke, the way they crafted their sentences, made people feel more comfortable buying their programs.

These sorts of techniques are obviously manipulative, but that's not necessarily a bad thing. Jeff & Kane were teaching really valuable techniques. In fact, they were *teaching* NLP as much as they were using it themselves. It's a way of communicating. It's a way of guiding people through a thought process. It's a way of running your business and Jeff & Kane were masters of it.

Visit **Keynote**Mastery.com to download worksheet #6 on NLP.

I started to run into Jeff in other places. He was speaking everywhere and so was I. He told me that he did most of the free "feeder" events and that Kane only came to mine because it was a large group. It was normally Jeff's responsibility to speak at the free events and get people to sign up for their initial $99 weekend workshops. In fact, he later told me that he spoke at 164 events in 2009, 17 more than me. To this day, I have never met anyone who spoke at more events than Jeff did in 2009.

He was curious about my business too. He knew I covered social media at a conference in Sweden and wanted to know more. He soon invited me to deliver my program at their next three-day workshop. It was an awesome experience. In a way, they reminded me of Edith Yeung. They were running a real business. Their event was in an impressive hotel conference room and they had a stage, fancy lavalier microphones, audiovisual people and staff at the back of the room. It was a professional production.

My presentation went extremely well. They asked if I had anything to sell but the only thing I had were those marketing CDs. I wasn't comfortable selling my first book and *Webify Your Business* wasn't complete at that point. I sold a few CDs and they let me keep all of the revenue because it was such a small amount of money anyway.

They invited me to come back and speak again at their next workshop in May, which was scheduled for the same day as my return flight from Stockholm. I wanted to do it and agreed to come. I told them I would be coming directly from San Francisco airport and they loved it. It made me that much more credible.

My flight arrived at SFO at about 11:00 AM and I took a taxi directly to the hotel where their event was taking place. My hair was a mess and my suitcases still had the luggage tags attached. They introduced me to the crowd and told everyone that I had just gotten off a plane from Sweden where I had delivered this same program for a large corporate audience. I walked on stage like a rockstar and everybody looked up at me with fascination in their eyes.

I brought almost 60 copies of my new *Webify Your Business* book to Sweden and still had 13 left in my suitcase. My session went well again and the books sold out immediately. Jeff & Kane were impressed, and I was thrilled with the $260 I earned in book sales. They invited me to come back again, and the relationship continued for the next 18 months.

It was clear that the business model required significant sales at those weekend workshops and allowing me to keep 100% of my revenue was a favor. Normally, they would ask for 50% but made an exception for me. They were apparently grossing over $100,000 in sales during their weekend workshops, and I had hardly any money at all. I was selling a $20 book, and they knew it wasn't worth splitting the revenue. Besides, I was getting the audience excited, which apparently made the next session particularly profitable.

I was obviously happy that they understood my situation, but I also realized that I really needed to have a more expensive product to sell. These two guys were making great money and it was all because of their sales. They had these expensive programs to sell and their attendees were buying. Even though I hated the idea, I was desperate for money and needed something of my own.

After brainstorming for ideas, I scheduled a full-day social media workshop in August and promoted it to my Meetup group. The whole day would be video recorded so that I could produce a DVD set with the footage. I told my members that they would not be able to ask questions and that the day would consist of six hour-long sessions, each on a different platform within the social media realm. Tickets were $25 each and they sold like hotcakes!

I had 86 people at the workshop. It was held in a large upstairs meeting room at the local library, and I had to keep the registration fee quiet because the rental agreement stipulated that all events had to be free. Nobody asked any questions and the event went well. At the end of the day, I told everyone that the final DVD product would sell for $299 but anyone who wanted to order one that day could get it for $100. Six people bought. I earned $2,750 that day. It was huge for me!

That event was valuable in other ways too. It established me as a local expert on social media, and all of my Meetup members now knew what I was doing. They all knew I had recently come back from Sweden (for the second time) and now saw the content I was sharing at these faraway conferences. I worked hard to prepare for that day and would soon have a legitimate product to sell at Jeff & Kane's events.

The final product was beautiful. I hired a company to package it together in an impressive black plastic container and made a 30-page workbook to accompany the DVDs. It was a nice package. It looked professional and I wanted to start selling them as soon as possible, but it never amounted to much. I just wasn't very good at platform selling. As I said, you need to have a certain mindset to do that well, and it definitely didn't come naturally to me.

Platform speaking requires complete confidence in yourself as well as your product or program. Some people are better at it than others. As always, practice makes perfect. You can get better at it. You can improve. But in the meantime, keynote speaking is still the ultimate prize and the branding is very different. Your odds of being paid to speak improve significantly when you position yourself as a corporate keynote speaker and leave the products and programs behind.

My working relationship with Jeff & Kane lasted until June, 2011, when they moved their business to Sydney, Australia. That market was apparently much more enthusiastic about self-help business events, while the American market had already been over-marketed for years by Tony Robbins and T. Harv Eker. Anyway, I learned a ton about the business and while platform speaking isn't a good fit for me, I will forever be grateful to Jeff & Kane for including me in their workshops. It was a blast.

ARUBA

After the 2008 Toastmasters speaking competition, I had become well known in the local Toastmasters community. I taught a session about podcasting at the 2008 fall conference and agreed to speak again at the 2009 spring conference. Meanwhile, a member of my Entrepreneur & Small Business Academy was holding an event the exact same day and wanted me to participate on a panel during the lunch hour.

It was a busy day. I had to be at the Toastmasters conference in the morning, drive across town for the lunch event in San Ramon and then go back to the Toastmasters conference for my afternoon session. It seemed like a pain in the neck at the time and I was tempted to cancel on the luncheon but decided against it … thank God!

The lunch panel went very well. They were all self-employed professionals and my guerrilla tactics were perfect for them. After the panel, I ate lunch quickly and was running out the door when Dale Hamakawa approached me. She was on the board of directors for the Society of Incentive Travel Executives (SITE) and they were looking for a social media speaker for their annual conference in Aruba. The conference was scheduled for November, 2009. Aruba?!

The emails started going back and forth and sure enough, they selected me to speak at the conference. They weren't going to pay me anything, but they covered all the travel expenses. I was going to Aruba! It was perfect.

Credit Card Balance: $29,536 (November, 2009)

The SITE Conference was amazing. From the moment I arrived until the moment I left, everything was taken care of. There were uniformed people at the baggage claim area with signs for SITE members. There were buses ready to take us from the airport to the hotel. People greeted us at the hotel entrance and ushered us from one event to the next throughout the conference. Everything was fancy. Everything was extravagant. Everything was paid for.

The SITE members who were attending the conference were all "incentive travel executives." So what does that mean? It means that these people all manage extravagant incentive trips for large corporations, involving hundreds of attendees and multi-million-dollar budgets. For the hosting destination, Aruba in this case, it was an enormous opportunity to impress these gatekeepers of multimillion-dollar budgets. They were trying to sell Aruba as a place where these corporate budgets could be spent.

In 2001, just nine days after 9/11, I went to Hawaii with a friend of mine. He worked at Sun Microsystems and had achieved their most ambitious sales targets, earning him a ticket to their elite "President's Club" incentive trip. He and a companion would be flown to Waikiki and treated like royalty for four days. Since he was single at the time, he invited me to be his companion. This was an incentive trip and I'm sure the whole thing cost millions.

Years earlier, I was still in the promotional products industry and one of my distributor friends landed a huge order for 1,000 K2 mountain bikes. They were all gifted to top producers at an annual sales convention in Colorado. It was a million-dollar order for him and that was only for the bikes. The company undoubtedly spent millions more on airfare, hotel, food and booze. This, too, was an incentive trip.

The people in Aruba sold those types of trips all day long. They controlled huge budgets and were used to fancy amenities, and Aruba delivered. We had torch-lit cocktail parties on the beach. We had a gala dinner in a huge building decorated with beautiful women wearing massive butterfly wings and their bodies painted bright colors, dancing gracefully on 12-foot-tall platforms. We had plated lunch service with keynote speakers, traditional dance performances and live marching bands.

There's an art to feeding hundreds of people who all need to be treated like royalty. Many of the events had huge tables with hundreds of fancy hors d'oeuvres or desserts in shot glasses, all perfectly lined up like little soldiers. In some cases, there were 10 or 15 food stations each serving sliced beef tenderloin, seared scallops or salmon fillets. Nicely dressed waiters wandered through the crowds with trays full of wine glasses.

I had never experienced such extravagance in my whole life. Was this what all large business conferences were like? I had worked dozens of tradeshows earlier in my career but had never gone to a conference like this before. As it turns out, this is standard fare for most corporate events, and I would later see similar extravagance at other events all around the world.

Predictably, my session went well. My social media program had a certain magic. It was new. It was exciting. It held the promise of new customers and new profits. My program was strong, and audiences usually reacted with enthusiasm and excitement. That's exactly what happened in Aruba. Despite their powerful contacts and massive budgets, they were commission salespeople in the end. They were self-employed professionals and they loved my approach.

I came home with renewed hope for what my career might lead to one day. Although the conference business was still reeling from the "AIG affect" of unjustified corporate extravagance, I had now experienced some of that opulence myself and wanted more. Meanwhile, the attendees all organized corporate events of their own and periodically hired speakers. In time, the SITE conference brought me spinoff opportunities in San Diego, the Napa Valley, Miami, Cancun, Grand Cayman and India.

GETTING PAID TO SPEAK

When you sign up as an organizer on Meetup.com, the basic account allows you to set up as many as three different groups. My primary group was the Entrepreneur & Small Business Academy, but I created a second one to attract potential new members to my Toastmasters club. It was an extremely effective tactic. We consistently had young, new prospective members visiting and joining our club, and they all found us on Meetup.

Within a couple of years, our Toastmasters club had almost 50 members, making it the third largest in the district. We also had a younger average age by a significant margin. As I mentioned earlier, much like Rotary, Kiwanis and Lions clubs, Toastmasters clubs tend to attract older people who are approaching, or are perhaps already at, retirement age. Our club was different. Most of our members were in their 30s, 40s or 50s, and many were successful professionals as well.

I credit two things. First, just as I had originally joined our club because Josh was there before me, so too did other younger people who came later. With each new youngish member, the probability of other younger visitors joining increased. Over time, the club membership became younger and more professional, attracting yet more young professional members.

Meetup was the second reason. In those early days, Meetup was still brand new and was attracting young tech-savvy people who were all exploring the platform in search of their own interests. I tagged that Meetup group with keyword phrases like "public speaking" and "professional speaker" and "motivational speaker," knowing those phrases would be searched for by people looking to improve their speaking skills. It worked like a charm.

I used the third group as an experiment. I called it the Meetup Speakers Bureau. I didn't know if I was allowed to do that or not, but nobody ever said anything and it attracted a steady stream of aspiring speakers. I never did anything with the group and planned to eventually replace it with something else until one day, I received an email from a woman at Grant Thornton, a large accounting firm with offices across the country, including downtown San Francisco. They were looking for a speaker.

I immediately called the woman and introduced myself. I guess the right thing to do would've been to notify everyone in the group and let them all apply for this opportunity, but I had to take my shot first. I needed the money and was excited at the prospect of potentially negotiating a real speaking fee for an event. I had never technically been paid to speak. Lennart Svanberg in Sweden paid me a percentage of his registration revenues, but that was essentially a revenue share. In this case, Grant Thornton was ready to pay a fixed fee to a professional speaker. The phone call went well and they asked for my fee. I had no idea what to say. Eventually, I asked for $2,500, and she said their budget was $1,500. That was fine with me!

Credit Card Balance: $29,746 (December, 2009)

The event took place in December, just a few days after I got back from Aruba, at the exclusive City Club in downtown San Francisco. I was still flying high from the Aruba trip and felt more legitimate than ever. I was an international speaker, after all. I had spoken in Sweden twice, Canada twice, Finland once and now in the Caribbean as well. And since this was a local event, I put my suit and tie on and took the Bay Area Rapid Transit (BART) into the city. It was fun to take public transportation to an event where I would get paid $1,500 to speak for just one hour!

My contact gave me an envelope with a check inside as soon as I arrived, and I went to the front to ensure my laptop was properly booted up and ready to go. The presentation went well, and I shook hands and exchanged cards with a number of people afterward: another success. I sat in disbelief on BART that evening, feeling like a rock star in disguise. There were plenty of other people on that train, but none of them knew what I had accomplished that day. I was smiling from ear to ear.

The early victories are often private victories. There's very little fanfare. Few people hear the details. You might be celebrating all by yourself, sitting in a public transportation train, but they are no less important. Give yourself that moment. Bask in the glory. Relive the victory a thousand times in your mind. There are plenty of struggles on the road to success and you need to relish those victories when they arrive.

33

REFERRAL MAGIC

2010 was a breakthrough year for me. When I contributed to Edith Yeung's BizTechDay in 2009, I made a contact who later introduced me to Kathleen Mozena, an account executive at Keynote Speakers, one of the largest speakers' bureaus on the west coast. It could've been the break I was waiting for. After our initial email introduction, I sent her copies of my two books along with all of my marketing material and held my breath, and she delivered.

Credit Card Balance: $33,244 (January, 2010)

With my new credential of speaking at the SITE Annual Conference in Aruba, Kathleen managed to get me into a Meeting Professionals International (MPI) event at the Moscone Center in January. It was another session on social media and she negotiated a fee of $2,000, $500 higher than Grant Thornton had paid me, but I wouldn't get the full $2,000. After Kathleen's 50% commission, I would only get $1,000 but I didn't care. It was another amazing opportunity for me and I was grateful to finally have a productive relationship with a speakers' bureau.

Speakers' bureaus normally take between 20% or 30% commission on speaking engagements they book. Generally speaking, if the speaking fee is $5,000 or less, they take 30%. If the speaking fee is between 5,000 and 20,000, they take 25% and for fees over 20,000, they take 20%. But my opportunity with MPI was different because I was only being paid $2,000, significantly less than their normal fees. Kathleen asked me if 50% would be acceptable and I eagerly accepted.

It was funny to me that $2,000 was apparently way below their normal minimum, but it was also the most I had ever been paid. I knew from years earlier that professional speakers get $5,000 or more for each event but to me, getting $2,000 for a one-hour speech still felt like robbery.

Anyway, the ball was starting to roll. People whom I met in Aruba had already contacted me about other events, and my new speakers' bureau contact had booked me already. Lennart Svanberg in Sweden had hired me five times so far and I was hoping for more. My social media program was hot and my career was definitely moving forward.

I also made a contact at the American Marketing Association (AMA) based in Chicago and was going there in March for my first session to their members. The topic? Social media, of course. They didn't pay me anything but covered my travel expenses and I was thrilled to add them to my list of clients.

While I was in Chicago, I received a call from a guy named Steve Diamond from Bloomberg TV in New York City. He wanted to have me speak at an event they were holding with a local cable affiliate. At first, I didn't believe it was real. I didn't understand the business model behind the event and was immediately skeptical of his intentions. How would he have found me? And what was their business model? It didn't make sense.

Kathleen Mozena from the bureau called me shortly after I got back from Chicago. She told me that she had an opportunity with Bloomberg TV in New York City. I told her about my call with Steve Diamond. She confirmed that it was indeed a real opportunity and they were inquiring about an event in Philadelphia on July 27th. I couldn't believe it. They would pay $5,000 and Kathleen would take 30%, leaving me with $3,500, another record.

Meanwhile, one of the people I met in Aruba was Rajeev Kohli from Creative Travel in India. We had been emailing back and forth ever since the conference, and he wanted me to share my social media program with two American Society of Travel Agents (ASTA) chapters in India. I was skeptical about this at first too, but the details became increasingly clear, and he eventually proposed an all-expenses paid eight-day travel itinerary in Rajasthan's "golden triangle" (including New Delhi, Agra and Jaipur), plus $3,000 to deliver two social media workshops in India. The travel dates were from July 14th to July 24th.

Rajeev's proposal arrived in the same week as the Bloomberg deal and left only two days in between the two commitments. On top of that, a referral from another past event led to an opportunity at the Mandalay Bay hotel in Las Vegas on July 7th for $4,500 plus travel expenses. That one also got confirmed around the same time.

In the speaking business, there are basically three parallel circuits. There's the "free circuit," the "cheap circuit" and the "pro circuit." The free circuit is free. You don't get paid anything to speak and earn money instead by selling stuff. The cheap circuit is where you get paid between $1,000 and $4,000 and the pro circuit is $5,000 and up.

Technically, I wouldn't make $5,000 on any one of these three opportunities. I would make $4,500 for the Vegas event. I would make $3,000 plus an all-expense-paid eight-day tour of New Delhi, Agra and Jaipur for the India events. And for the Bloomberg event, they would indeed be paying $5,000, but I would only net $3,500. Even still, they all struck me as clear pro-circuit gigs. I had been building my speaking career for over three years and had never once had a pro-circuit gig. Now, all of a sudden, I had three in *one* month!

Things happen in clusters. Much later in 2013, I had 31 paid speaking engagements during that year. I booked five of them on the same day! It always seems to be this way. Your business might be in a holding pattern for months or even years but then all of a sudden, a string of victories happen in quick succession. The Chinese bamboo tree works the same way. You can water the ground for five years without seeing a thing. But once the stalk finally breaks the surface, it can grow up to 80 feet in just six weeks.

ANXIETY

The weight of the situation started to build. My three pro-circuit gigs all got confirmed during March of 2010. I didn't notice the changes at first. I chalked it up to being more social and enjoying the fruits of my labor. I was drinking more and eating more as well. I thought everything was fine, until it happened.

Credit Card Balance: $35,525 (April, 2010)

Something snapped in April. I remember it like it was yesterday: anxiety. I woke up one morning and felt like my feet weren't touching the floor and I was panicking to make contact. I wanted to feel something solid. I felt like I was submerged in water without being able to swim. When I was a child, I was a poor swimmer and always felt panicky in the water. I desperately wanted to grab onto something solid but, of course, found nothing sturdy in the water. This felt the same way. I was panicky. I needed to feel grounded but felt instead like I was being swept along by the wind.

I had a panic attack once before in my life. It was 2004 and I was in the middle of a crazy day of appointments all over town with time constraints at every turn. In the latter half of the afternoon, I was driving along highway 24 towards Walnut Creek to drop off an escrow package and would then have to turn around and drive all the way back to San Francisco(about 20 miles away) to meet a friend who was visiting from Vancouver. Yet again, for the third or fourth time that day, I was behind schedule and was hitting traffic on the road.

It started right there as I sat behind the wheel. I got that panicky feeling and my head started spinning. My breaths became shallow and everything appeared to get dislodged from the anchoring.

It's a difficult thing to describe. In regular life, most things around you appear stable. They're essentially fixed, at least for the moment. The wall is in one place. It's not moving. The TV is sitting in one place, the couch is in one place and the coaster on the cof-fee table is in one place. These are things you don't have to worry about. They're just sitting there. No big deal. The only things you have to worry about are the things that are moving.

Well, when that panicky feeling started, it felt like everything was moving and nothing was fixed anymore. Imagine that. It means you have to worry about everything now. You can't count on anything anymore. Everything is moving and nothing is fixed. Now, the entire world is a danger zone and you don't have control over anything. You're just sitting there, waiting for something to hit you. That's what it felt like.

I pulled over on the side of the highway and put my hazard lights on. I tried to take some deep breaths but felt like my rib cage was too tight to allow my lungs to expand. I stayed there for a few moments and decided that I needed to keep going. Every minute I stayed there would make me even more late for my two remaining appointments. I got to Walnut Creek in one piece and dropped off the escrow package. One down, one to go.

When I got back on the highway to drive back to San Francisco, the traffic was much better going west, the counter-commute direc-tion. That helped, but I still felt panicky and frantic. I did eventu-ally make it to the city and met up with my friend. I told him I was in bad shape, and we sat on his hotel's rooftop pool terrace and had a cigarette. I made it to my last appointment for the day, and things were slowing down inside my head. Within the next hour or two, the panicky feeling disappeared completely and didn't come back until April 2010.

As soon as I woke up, I recognized the feeling. It was like an old friend had come back to visit, or actually an old enemy. The panicky feeling was there again. The frantic thoughts and shallow breaths; they all felt oddly familiar. I didn't know what was wrong, but my instincts were incredibly clear. I needed to regain a sense of control. I needed something to grab onto.

What ended up becoming the subject of my control imperative? My health. I needed to stop drinking alcohol, stop eating simple carbohydrates, stop drinking coffee and start going for walks each evening to calm my mind down. I've never had such a clear and urgent push towards healthy living, but it seemed like the only thing I could do to reduce the panicky feelings.

I was 182 lbs. when this all started, the heaviest I have ever weighed. When the anxiety came into my life, my diet changed dramatically and I lost 16 lbs. in just three weeks. It helped a little, but the panicky feeling didn't go away. I did sleep better and felt a bit more in control, but there were many things that remained strange. I was afraid of the dark, something I hadn't felt since I was a child. I was nervous when I was home alone at night and also when I was walking at night after the sun had gone down.

During the previous several years, my life seemed very stressful. I was failing to live up to my own potential. I was unable to achieve a "lifestyle commensurate with my skillset," and I was still single as well. All of these cumulative failures had left me in a frantic and stressful state of mind, but it turned out that failure wasn't nearly as stressful as success.

When I was a failure, nobody was watching. It was just me. Very few people even took notice. I was the only one who realized how horrible things were. But now, with three pro-circuit gigs booked in a single month, just three months away, I was about to have a lot more eyeballs on my life. Now, people were paying me good money to speak at their events. Now, the lights were on me. I had to deliver. I couldn't let these people down. I had to deliver at the level that was expected of a professional speaker. Did I have the credibility? Did I deserve to be the one speaking at the front of the room? Would I be good enough to satisfy the event organizers? I was scared to death.

Regardless of where you might be on your journey, believe me, success is a lot more stressful than failure. Failure sucks but it's not actually that stressful. It's lonely. It's frustrating. It messes with your head, but it's not stressful in the same way that success is. When people are relying on you, it introduces a level of stress that I never experienced before, and it took almost two years for it to go away.

The good news is that it did eventually subside. Persian Sufi poets correctly point out that "this too shall pass." After 20 months of anxiety, it left my life as quickly as it arrived. I woke up one morning in early January, 2012, just a few days after the stressful holiday season was over, and it was gone. I knew it immediately. My mind was crisp. The haze was gone and my feet felt like they were firmly on the floor.

I remember that morning clearly. I doubted it at first but as the day went by, I continued to feel good. I felt strong, actually, and felt strong again the next day and the next and the next. The anxiety never came back in the same way. I still had times that put me on my heels, but that frantic helpless feeling had vanished.

A million things happened during that 20-month period and I'll tell you about many of them, but the lesson is that these things take time. They are seasons in your life and it takes time for them to pass through. You don't pivot in a day. You don't adjust immediately. It takes time to get used to shifting realities in your life and you need to be patient with yourself.

I'm sure there will be other phases in my life that will bring the anxiety back. I'm sure I will go through this again. But next time, I will know that it's a phase. It's just my mind and my body adjusting to new realities and it takes time to fully make these transitions. You may go through this too. Be gentle with yourself and trust that it will pass.

THE SECRET

Credit Card Balance: $37,399 (May, 2010)

My weight had stabilized at 166lbs. by mid-May. The anxiety was just a month old at this point. It was brutal, but it was also becoming a bit more familiar to me. I was finding ways to deal with it. My pro-circuit month was just six weeks away, and I had another important gig in Palm Springs on June 11th. That was my next hurdle and I was very concerned about how I would hold up.

When I accepted the invitation for that event, I agreed to drive down instead of booking a flight, saving the client airfare and also some expensive taxi or airport shuttle rides. But at that time, I was driving a horrible old beat-up car that would *never* make the trip. I had been broke for so long that my mode of transportation had diminished to almost nothing at all. The only way to do the trip was to rent a car.

About the same time, Josh had been going to the local library and taking out audio books on CD and listening to them in his car. I decided to do the same thing for my trip to Palm Springs. The library had many audio books on CD and I checked out three of them, including *The Secret*. It was a book I had heard so much about, originally from that Meetup event I attended three years earlier, and I was looking forward to seeing what all the fuss was about.

The day of the big trip, I picked up a white Nissan Altima and put my bags and laptop in the trunk and the CD audio books in the passenger seat. I got on the freeway and put the first CD of *The Secret* in the CD player. The book began, and the fog in my brain immediately started to clear.

The book made so much sense. In my frantic state of anxiety, its message was crystal clear. Everything in my life was a function of my own thinking. Indeed, my thoughts were *becoming* things in my life, good and bad, mostly bad. I was so freaked out about my evolving career, my mounting credit card debts and a host of other issues and neuroses; all were perpetuating bad things in my life.

I was noticing everything negative in my life and making a bad situation worse. I needed to start thinking about the good things and the things I had some control over. I needed to think about the vision I had for my future. I needed to imagine myself succeeding at these upcoming pro-circuit gigs, not failing. I needed to see myself victorious amidst all those challenges.

I listened to those CDs the whole way down. My mind became calmer and calmer with each passing track. The book was like a revelation to me. I'm not sure it would've had the same effect if I wasn't struggling with anxiety, but given that fact, it was the perfect medicine. A tiny glimpse of confidence came back to my life that day, and I felt empowered to get through the event in Palm Springs.

My diet was my first weapon against anxiety and *The Secret* was my second. It was a discovery that literally changed my life because it led to a subscription on Audible.com and an addiction to audio books that has since included literally hundreds of titles. The book didn't erase my anxiety any more than the weight loss did, but both helped me cope. Both helped me manage the feelings I was experiencing and get through the things I needed to do in my life. Both helped me be more optimistic and drive my career forward.

> I strongly recommend listening to positive audio programs in your daily life. *The Secret* is a great place to start, but there are many excellent programs by Tony Robbins, Jim Rohn and Brian Tracy among others. You may find them cheesy. I felt that way for years. But if you listen to them with an open mind, they can literally shift the way you think and provide powerful insights into the way your mind works.

PHYLLIS

B ack in early 2006, the man who lived in the condominium below me moved out and Phyllis moved in. A Jewish woman about 20 years my senior, she enjoyed her cocktails and cigarettes just like me. I didn't quit smoking until October of that year. Anyway, her patio was directly beneath mine and we were frequently out there at the same time, enjoying a drink and a smoke. It wasn't long before we became friends.

I was in the middle of my struggle back then, and Phyllis had her own set of challenges and frustrations. I've always been a very open communicator and regularly shared my frustrations with her and, of course, that encouraged her to do the same. The whole thing quickly evolved into a trusting friendship. She was my confidant. I could tell her anything and she never judged or took sides. She was never condescending or patronizing like so many of my other friends. It was refreshing and I was grateful.

When you're struggling financially, at least in my case, it's the socializing that's the first to go. It was embarrassing to hang out with my other friends. They all had regular jobs and were making progress, slowly but surely, in their lives. They were getting a paycheck every two weeks. Meanwhile, I felt like I was on a hamster wheel, running frantically but making no progress at all.

They would ask me "How are you doing?" and I would cringe at the thought of responding. I was struggling. That's all there was to it. Things were not going well and I was embarrassed to admit it. Actually, I was indeed making progress but it hadn't changed my lifestyle yet. I was still financially struggling, just like before. That was the problem. I was making progress, but nobody could see it. I was the only person who saw the steps I was taking.

With Phyllis, it was different. I didn't have to worry about any of that. It wasn't a competition and she was sufficiently fascinated by my audacious career choice that she listened to my stories without judgement. I could tell her about all the latest developments, even though I was still eating two chicken thighs, a yam and half a head of broccoli each evening for dinner. My victories and my failures could co-exist at the same time.

Today, I know she thought I was crazy. We're still friends, and she's told me many times that she never thought I'd pull this off. Like so many others, she didn't even realize that a career as a professional speaker existed. She had no idea how much money speakers can make and certainly never thought that struggling Patrick who lived upstairs would ever make that kind of money himself. But at the time, she pretended to believe it was possible just to keep the conversation going. She enjoyed hearing about my escapades and adventures, and they were getting more interesting as time went on.

Phyllis and I had a few things in common. We both had frustrations with our parents and struggles in other areas of our lives, and we were both willing to admit them. Many people have struggles, but few are willing to talk about them, much less consider the possibility that they might be part of the problem themselves. We're all the largest factors in our own lives. The things that are going well in your life are most likely the result of your own good decisions along the way, and the things that are going poorly are the result of your bad decisions. Most people are unwilling to take that critical look at themselves. Not only were Phyllis and I both willing to take that look, but we were also willing to discuss it with each other.

Brené Brown delivered a brilliant TED Talk about vulnerability and shame, and it's an area I'm very passionate about. Most people view vulnerability as a sign of weakness but I disagree. I view vulnerability as a sign of courage. It takes courage to look critically at yourself and consider how you might be affecting your own situation. It takes even more courage to then share those observations with others. But when you do, it leads to very strong connections between people.

I'm certainly not saying that I'm unusually strong or that Phyllis is unusually strong either, but there's a harsh honesty to our conversations. We're both willing to face the cold, hard truth and take personal responsibility for our lives. It's just a way of thinking, that's all. Some people think this way. Most people don't. For those who do, it translates into emotional depth that other people never experience.

Some people live in the shallow end of the pool, and others live in the deep end of the pool. That's fine, except for the fact that those in the shallow end honestly believe they're in the deep end. They have no idea what the deep end is actually like. They've never experienced it before. And if you try to describe it to them, they have no idea what you're talking about. It's like describing air to a fish.

I've met plenty of people in the shallow end and on some occasions, I've spent hours trying to explain the difference to them, but they just don't get it. They think I always want to talk about negative things or that I want them to have problems even when they don't, but neither of those is true. Instead, I enjoy talking about and fully understanding a problem before arriving at a solution. Solutions end conversations. As soon as a solution has been presented, there's nothing left to talk about.

In his book *7 Habits of Highly Effective People,* Stephen Covey says "Seek first to understand, then to be understood." The key to effective communication is listening and asking probing questions to learn more and understand the other person's situation. What does the world look like through their eyes? Don't be in a rush to present solutions all the time. The most meaningful conversations are about the challenges and frustrations.

I knew a girl once who was always "excellent" or "perfect." No matter what day it was, she was constantly in a great mood. "Never better!" That's fine, and I'm happy for her, but I don't believe it for a second. Besides, if you're always in a great mood, how will I know when you're *actually* having a good day? When I'm having a good day, believe me, you'll know. And if I'm frustrated about something, you'll know that as well. It's life, and I want to share it with the people I'm close to.

Let me also say that the shallow end isn't a bad place to be. Many highly successful CEOs, executives, salespeople and athletes are in that category. Solution-oriented people are doers. They get stuff done. They waste no time talking about problems. It's awesome, but I need more than that. I appreciate solutions as much as anyone, but I need to fully understand the problem as well. And ironically, it's that same approach that makes me a good speaker. I always explore the problems my audiences are facing and that pulls them in. They feel understood and are then more open to my input and suggestions. I'm grateful for that.

These differences are huge. People in the shallow end sometimes oversimplify things and want short, direct conversations. People in the deep end relish complexity and enjoy long philosophical discussions. People in the shallow end want quick, clean answers. People in the deep end incorporate nuances and subtleties in their suggestions. People in the shallow end usually think people in the deep end are crazy, and people in the deep end have no way to defend themselves against those accusations. These are two entirely different species within the human race and they rarely communicate well with each other. I'm clearly in the deep end. Where are you?

Not surprisingly, people in the deep end are also more likely to experience depression and anxiety. I don't think I've ever been depressed. A friend once described it as a feeling of hopelessness. I've never felt hopeless, but starting in April 2010, I experienced a true episode of anxiety in my life, and Phyllis had dealt with those emotions in her own life. So during my 20-month bout with anxiety, Phyllis was a valuable sounding board. I had never dealt with those emotions before, and she helped navigate me through. She didn't make me feel broken or inferior. She just listened and offered advice.

My mother had these emotions as well and like me, she looked for ways to deal with them. She took walks almost every day, and I now understand why she did that. I felt a compulsion to do the same thing when I felt frantic and out of control. But one thing my mother refused to do was take prescription medication or visit a psychologist or psychiatrist. Those things were for crazy people, and she wasn't about to put herself in that bucket.

Phyllis felt differently. Her father was a chemist and knew every ingredient in every pharmaceutical medication, and Phyllis is exactly the same way. She knows the science and is an advocate for the impact these medications can have on your life. Of course, I naturally followed in my mother's footsteps and instinctively resisted medication. When I met Phyllis, she challenged those views and encouraged me to think differently.

I still believe that pharmaceutical medication should be minimized and avoided if possible, but I also acknowledge that medications can improve your quality of life. The one medication that Phyllis advocated for me was Ativan. It's fairly mild, but can calm my brain when I need to get some rest. Sleep was the primary requirement for me. When I had an important event coming up, I couldn't sleep properly and would lie in bed for hours waiting for the sun to come up again. Ativan eliminated that nightmare for me.

Remember those sleepless nights in Stockholm? That was before Ativan. What about the sleepless night before the BizTechDay conference? That was before Ativan. Or the sleepless night in Aruba? That was before Ativan.

I don't take this stuff often, but when I have an early morning speaking engagement or an eight-hour time change to deal with, I don't fool around anymore. I need the rest. I can't tell you how many times I've spoken in front of respectable audiences after having had absolutely no sleep. I can do it, but it's difficult and I need a day or two to recover afterwards. Ativan solves this problem.

Phyllis deserves credit for many things. She followed my journey as a professional speaker more than anyone else. I've called her countless times from airports and hotels around the world. She heard all the stories and provided support on a million different occasions. But she also deserves credit for shifting my opinion on Rx medication. It has improved my quality of life.

If you struggle with anxiety in your life, do something about it. I believe that my mother's anxiety contributed to the incapacitated state she's in today. She can no longer speak and is constantly immersed in fear and confusion. I believe her anxiety made her crazy, and I'm not about to let the same thing happen to me. There is good medication available that can help, not to mention yoga, meditation, healthy eating and taking walks. It's up to you to manage your mental state. Don't let your pride stand in the way.

THE PRO CIRCUIT

The time had come. I had three pro-circuit gigs in a single month, and that month had finally arrived. The lights were on. It was show time. My trip to Vegas was a resounding success. The event was for the National Association of Healthcare Recruiters (NAHCR) and it had over 500 people, almost exclusively women, in attendance. My session went extremely well, and I had a huge lineup after my session of people who wanted to buy my book. I sold 66 books that day, each for $20, and most people paid cash. That meant I ended up with over $1,000 cash in my pocket and a huge smile on my face. I even asked a guy to record the whole thing with my FLIP digital video recorder, and I later compiled clips of that footage into my first "demo reel" video.

The trip to India was a success as well. Actually, all three events went well that month, but India was a challenge for many reasons. It was my first trip to a true developing country, and I had had 12 inoculation shots in the weeks prior to the trip, protecting me from diseases I didn't even recognize. And even though the shots were intended to make me safer, they also served to instill the fear of God in my psyche.

Malaria was the worst one. I couldn't get immunized against it and the medication was known to cause nightmares and possible psychological side effects. With my anxiety just three months old at this point, I didn't need any psychological side effects making things worse. I carried the medication with me but never took it, making me even more nervous about possibly getting sick.

Also, on Rajeev's advice, I went through a complicated (and expensive) process to get a tourist VISA even though I was going for business reasons and had 50 books in my suitcase. The last thing I needed was to get stopped at customs with the wrong VISA. Thankfully, that obstacle passed without incident.

Then there were the pickup arrangements. I arrived at about midnight and was instructed to look for a driver at the airport. I had never had instructions like that before and when I arrived, there was a scrum of drivers at least 10 people deep, all looking for their respective passengers. When I finally connected with mine and got my bags from baggage claim, we went outside into the hot muggy New Delhi night and walked to the car with stray dogs roaming about and chaotic traffic all around us.

Everything about the experience was intense. The things you see, the things you smell, the things you touch, the things you taste—they were all intense. But that is India. "Incredible India" was the tagline in the VISA office back in San Francisco, and it was a perfect description. India was incredible indeed, and I got treated like gold the whole time. Rajeev Kohli had taken care of everything and I was on the ride of my life.

I could tell you hundreds of individual stories about India, but it wouldn't add much to this memoir. To summarize, I stayed at incredible hotels, ate lots of Indian food, saw the sights, rode an elephant, bought an authentic hukka and took 26 videos during my stay. Suffice it to say, it was an amazing experience, and I am forever grateful to Rajeev and his colleagues at Creative Travel and ASTA. I've posted a few of those videos here:

http://www.keynotemastery.com/india/

Once I got back to California, I only had two days before my trip to Philadelphia for the Bloomberg event and decided to split the time difference between India and Philadelphia and stay on that schedule for the ensuing days. I went to sleep at 4:00 PM and got back up at midnight. My hope was to minimize the jet lag for my next event, and it worked perfectly. My flight to Philadelphia left at 6:00 AM, and I had already eaten lunch by then!

Shortly after I arrived in Philadelphia, I checked into my hotel, took a shower, put my suit back on and met Steve and Dave for the first time. Steve was the guy who called me when I was in Chicago, and Dave was the account executive for the northeast region of the country. I had just returned from India two days earlier and was sure to let them know. It all served to make me more credible as a speaker.

The Bloomberg event rocked. The audience was full of self-employed professionals and small business owners. My approach was perfect for them and I could feel the energy building as I walked them through my case histories. By the end, the whole room was buzzing and at least a dozen people came up after to ask questions or comment on my presentation. I could see Steve and Dave at the back of the room; smiling broadly and shaking hands with the event organizers. I had succeeded beyond my most optimistic expectations.

Bloomberg TV became my #1 client for the following five years—still to this day, in fact. My social media program was continuing to deliver, and I was getting better and better at playing the role of a professional speaker. I tried to act like a visiting diplomat. That was always the vision in my head and it was great at guiding my behavior. What would a visiting diplomat do? I strived to be kind, elegant and gracious. It was the perfect metaphor.

I got back home late on the 27th and was floating on a cloud. Everything had gone well. I was exhausted but had also managed to pull it off. It was over and I was home again. The whole thing seemed surreal and took weeks to fully sink in. I was an international speaker. There was no debate about that anymore. And although it would end up taking me over six months to collect the money from ASTA in India, I got paid by NAHCR and Bloomberg quickly and had some money in the bank. Things were looking up.

38

WAR STORIES

T hings continued to improve and I finally started making a little bit of money. There were dozens of bizarre situations along the way and there's no point telling all of those stories, but a few are worth mentioning. As a speaker, you end up in a lot of unique situations. As employees, most people go to the same workplace and see the same people every day. In my case, the situation is always different and you quickly learn to expect the unexpected.

Credit Card Balance: $20,885 (February, 2011)

I had a gig in Toronto in February 2011. It was a large human resources (HR) conference with over 4,000 attendees. My flight itinerary transferred through Chicago and there was a major blizzard moving into the area. My flight from Chicago was one of the last ones to get out. We landed in Toronto before the snow started falling but that changed quickly. My session was scheduled for 7:30 AM the following morning.

It's funny to see how different professions schedule their conferences. For self-employed and small business audiences, things rarely get going before 9:00 AM. Insurance conferences are even worse. They sometimes don't get started until 10:00 AM. Meanwhile, this HR conference started with a continental breakfast that opened at

6:30 AM. I spoke at another HR conference a year later and it was the same way.

There's an interesting distinction in the Middle East. Public sector events start late and are usually done by 2:00 PM. The public sector is full of local Arabs, while the private sector is comprised mostly of expats from India and Europe. The Arabs don't work that hard. They're done by mid-afternoon, but the expats are the opposite. They get up early and stay late.

The GCC region is very interesting. With so much oil wealth, the biggest player in all of their economies is the government, and the richest people are the local Arabs. If they're affiliated with the ruling family, they're loaded. But even if not, the government jobs pay lavish salaries for modest work and most of those jobs are reserved for local Arabs. The net result is an entitlement culture among the Arabs and a fairly lax work ethic.

In Dubai, Arabs only make up about 15% of the population. 85% are expats. Many of them are manual laborers from North Africa, Pakistan and Bangladesh but there's also a thriving business class comprised mostly of Indians and a few Europeans and Russians. Anyway, the Indians operate very differently from the Arabs. They keep the same hours as HR professionals in America (and Canada) while the Arabs are more like insurance agents.

The reasonable hour of 7:30 AM in Toronto is the same as 4:30 AM in California, and I hate mornings to begin with. Being self-employed and working from home, I never set my alarm unless I have a morning flight or a meeting to get to. Otherwise, I wake up whenever I wake up. Now, don't start thinking that I sleep all day. That's not true either. I usually wake up at 7:00 or 7:30 and am in front of my computer by 8:00, but it's not mandatory. Anyway, this was a perfect example where an Ativan helped me get some sleep before my morning session.

When I woke up in Toronto, over a foot of snow had fallen overnight. Dozens of flights had been cancelled the night before and the snow was still falling. I walked over the elevated walkway between the InterContinental Hotel and the Metro Toronto Convention Centre and looked out at the thick white blanket covering the railway tracks. It looked like a desolate place out there, and I had no idea how many people would attend my session.

My room was set up for 300 and we ended up with about 140. That's pretty impressive, actually. I was expecting 30 or 40. You just never know what you'll come across in this business. Things can go wrong. Sometimes it's the weather, sometimes it's something else. As a speaker, your job is to deliver the best possible session with the circumstances you find yourself in.

I did an event in Windsor, Canada (right across from Detroit), and my luggage never made it. I arrived the night before and knew my luggage would never arrive before my session the next morning. The hotel gave me a toothbrush and an incredibly tiny tube of toothpaste and I walked on stage wearing my jeans and a black sports jersey. It was an audience of about 200 municipal government employees and the first thing I said to them was: "Good morning, everyone. My luggage is in Chicago." Everyone laughed and the session went well after that.

It's important to acknowledge the obvious in these situations. Everyone sees that there's a problem. Everyone knows that something is wrong. There's no point pretending it's not there. People are actually quite forgiving when you're open and honest about the situation. They instinctively empathize with your predicament and cut you some slack as a result.

Now, if the predicament isn't obvious, there's no point mentioning it. If no one will notice either way, just let it go. Don't apologize for something when the audience doesn't even notice that there's a problem. But if the issue is obvious to everyone in the room, I like to acknowledge it head on. Of course, there are exceptions.

I did an event in Muscat, Oman, once and ended up offending a government minister. Oman is right beside Saudi Arabia and Yemen and shares many of the same regional cultures. After my session, I was invited to meet with a top-ranking government minister who was in charge of a significant portion of the country's public sector. This was an important meeting, not only for me but also for the conference planners who brought me to Oman.

My host was originally from India but had moved to Oman early in life. Her name is Mini Mary John. No joke. These names amaze me sometimes. Lennart Svanberg brought me to Sweden, Ali Al Kamali brought me to Dubai, Raveej Kohli brought me to India and Mini Mary John brought me to Oman. You can't make this stuff up! Anyway, it was important to Mini that the meeting go well.

After checking in with the security desk, we were escorted in to the minister's office. He was kind and welcoming and invited us to sit down. He and I began speaking about technology trends and the role they could play in Oman's public service. The minister asked a young Indian staffer to prepare some traditional Omani tea (which is similar to American coffee) and dates, and he returned soon thereafter with a white tray with small white cups, each filled with the tea.

The visiting diplomat metaphor was fresh in my mind and I tried to handle the situation gracefully. But without thinking, I took one of the cups with my left hand. Big mistake. In many Middle Eastern and South Asian cultures, the left hand is reserved for cleaning yourself after going to the bathroom—#2—and should never be used for handling food or drink. It's not uncommon to see people with their left hands literally behind their backs while eating food with their right hands.

Contrary to popular western stereotypes, people in the Middle East are incredibly kind and hospitable. Nobody said anything when I made my faux pas, but Mini was quick to point it out after we left. For those familiar with Middle Eastern culture, this would've been an insult. Since I was from America and the minister knew it was my first trip to Oman, I'm sure he was not offended. Nevertheless, I had demonstrated my ignorance and didn't even realize it at the time.

I felt very bad. I never meant to insult or offend anyone. In fact, I was trying hard to be respectful. I wish I could've apologized in person but never had that opportunity. These are the risks of international travel. Every place has its own cultures and traditions, and I'm learning as I go.

A similar thing happened in Paris. I made a fool of myself at the breakfast buffet. I was trying to eat a soft-boiled egg but did it all wrong, while a French woman stared in disbelief. I cracked the top of the shell with my knife but had to peel the whole thing with my fingers, burning myself in the process. I then put the whole thing in my mouth because I was worried the liquid yolk would spill everywhere, but it was still really hot, so I had to tilt my head back and forth and leave my mouth partially open to let the heat escape. Meanwhile, a nearby French couple was gracefully scooping out the contents of their eggs with tiny spoons. I obviously would've loved to do it that way but was afraid to break the surface. I had no choice! It was either me or the egg, and the egg lost.

Then there was Trinidad. I was invited to cover social media for a network marketing company. Some people call it multi-level marketing. I arrived near dinnertime and was greeted by a large Irish man at the airport. He told me that he was in charge of the security detail and if I followed his directions, everything would be fine. What was *that* all about? It turned out that a number of previous distributors felt cheated by the company and were now out for revenge. For every event the company held, they had tight security in place.

The extent of security was unprecedented for me. There were three security guards who were brought in from Ireland and then another four that were hired locally in Trinidad. We had our own vehicles and our own drivers. Also, the event was held in a different hotel than the one we were staying in. At night while we slept in our rooms, there were security guards sitting in chairs in the hallways. You would think this level of security would make you feel safer, but that's not how it felt for me. It actually felt a lot scarier.

I was driven to the hotel, and the Irish man spoke with someone at reception and then handed me a key to a room that had been reserved for me. The company had apparently checked into all of their rooms, including mine, when they first arrived. Anyway, the rest of the team was at a restaurant and I was supposed to meet them there. I had only 25 minutes to take a shower, shave and put a suit on, and then meet the Irish man and the driver in the lobby to drive to the restaurant.

When I got up to my floor, there was a privacy hanger on the door of "my" room. What should I do? I now only had 23 minutes left. I opened the door and the room was already occupied. There was nobody there, but the bed was unmade and there was an open suitcase on the floor and a laptop on the desk. I felt extremely uncomfortable but also had no easy way of addressing the problem. I had no idea where the Irish man had gone and needed to get cleaned up to meet with him again in 23 minutes. I needed a shower and decided to get it done as quickly as I could.

The hotel was fancy and the shower was essentially a glass enclosure that separated the bathroom area from the bedroom area. Three of the shower's four walls were glass from floor to ceiling. It was incredibly nerve-racking to take my clothes off and step into the shower. I felt like I was standing in a fishbowl. There's always that one point when you have soap on your face and can't even open your eyes. If someone walked in at that point, they would freak out for sure! The first thing they would see is a naked man with soap on his face, showering in their hotel room. Ugh! It was awful.

I did manage to get cleaned up, change my clothes and repack my suitcase and was only five minutes late in the lobby. I told the Irish man about the situation and he apologized about it but also smirked with a broad grin. When we arrived at the restaurant, there were six people sitting around the table. They were extremely casual and were all having a good time. I introduced myself and then explained that I had showered in one of their rooms. The room belonged to a guy who was, by far, the most paranoid and privacy-obsessed person in the group. I supposed Murphy's Law would guarantee that I ended up in *his* room. He was clearly uncomfortable, but the rest of the group erupted with laughter.

When we returned from the restaurant, I got my own room and got settled. These things almost always work out in the end, but I was getting used to the unpredictable nature of my speaking career. You just never know what circumstances you'll find at your next event, and it's best to roll with the punches wherever possible.

BOOK PUBLISHING

2011 was also the year that I published my third book with John Wiley & Sons, a large and respected national publisher. This was a huge achievement as it brought me out of the self-publishing world and gave me the credibility of being published by a traditional publisher. Like so many other milestones, I thought this one would finally solidify my career. And it was indeed a significant step, but I've learned many times that these steps are rarely homeruns. The vast majority are base hits.

The process actually started in 2010 when I sent proposals to 51 literary agents across the country. Eight expressed interest and I ended up working with Michael Larsen right here in San Francisco. He's a nationally recognized agent and did *Guerrilla Marketing* by Jay Conrad Levinson, among many other titles. He focused on nonfiction books and his wife, Elizabeth, focused on fiction titles.

My original pitch was to publish an updated version of *Webify Your Business,* but the big New York publishers had no interest in publishing a second edition of a self-published book. They wanted a new title. The result was *Marketing Shortcuts for the Self-Employed.* In the end, Wiley bought the deal and they picked the new title as well as the cover design. Yes, I was given an opportunity to veto certain versions, but it was clear that the driving force was coming from corporate.

Credit Card Balance: $9,816 (June, 2011)

The book was released in June, 2011. *Webify Your Business* had 60 chapters and I removed six because they were already out of date. I then added 26 new chapters so the finished product had 80 chapters. Just like *Webify Your Business,* the chapters were very short, just two or three pages long, and each one ended with an itemized to-do list. Those to-do lists were the most popular feature so I knew I had to keep them for this updated version.

The net result was that it looked like I had authored three different books. In fact, my first book was the compilation of my seven CDs, and my second was the compilation of my 52-week email course, plus eight more chapters. This third book was actually just an updated version of my second book. Yes, I added 26 new chapters and also did a huge edit of the original text, but the base content was largely an overlap of the previous title.

It's interesting because the effort of writing *this* book feels like the first time I've written a full book with the *intention* of writing a book. Once published, this will be my fourth book, but it feels like my first.

I actually wrote three other short handbooks before my first full-length book. I wrote *The Complete Employment Guide* back in 1994, immediately after graduating from university. It was a 31-page book that I sold with a CD included for $10 at Canadian universities across Ontario. Looking back now, it was my first information product and I sold over 1,000 copies!

In 2003, I wrote *Strategies for Seller Financing: A Guide to the Secondary Market for Business Notes* and used it to market myself as a note broker. It was 20 pages long and I printed 2,000 copies and sent them to business brokers across the United States. It had my contact information on the back cover and my phone rang for years with questions and inquiries. It was a feast-or-famine business and I abandoned the effort after a year, but the book campaign showed me the value of demonstrating my expertise in the public domain. It showed me the value of writing.

In 2005, I wrote *Loans & Lenders: A Guide for Buyers & Borrowers,* which was all about mortgages. I got my real estate license in 2004 and did the same thing I had done with business notes two years earlier. When I had those horrible workshops at the Oakland Marriott, I would give all of the attendees a copy of this little handbook. I also gave similar workshops at adult education programs and handed them out there as well. Unfortunately, the effort never yielded any real results.

There was a big difference between *Strategies for Seller Financing* and *Loans & Lenders*. The first was sent to business brokers. These were professionals who were helping business owners sell their businesses to new owners. My handbook could help them grow their own businesses. It was a resource that supported their own efforts. They had a built-in incentive to use it and potentially refer business to me.

Loans & Lenders was 27 pages long and was given to homeowners. These people weren't in business for themselves. They were just ordinary people and had tons of choice when selecting a mortgage broker. For them, my handbook was just a marketing piece and had no value as a business resource. To make matters worse, the recipients weren't sophisticated people, on average, so much of the content was beyond their curiosity anyway. They didn't really care about any of that stuff. They just wanted the lowest rate they could find, that's all.

If you're going to write a book, I highly recommend writing something that business people can leverage in their own businesses. You want your book to be a resource for your readers. Ideally, you want them to have a built-in incentive to read it and use it. Perhaps they can lower expenses with your advice, or perhaps they can grow revenue. Maybe they can lower employee turnover or increase innovation. Take some time to think about how your book will be used by its readers.

Obviously, *this* book is designed for people who want to become keynote speakers. Yes, it's a memoir, but it's also chock-full of advice you can use as you develop your own career. In fact, I think the advice in this book could be used by any self-employed professional. The journey I've traveled and the lessons I've learned along the way are all things that self-employed professionals go through themselves. That's my hope as I write these words. I want this book to be a valuable resource for people who are 100% responsible for their own income and who are building their careers, one step at a time, just like me.

Visit KeynoteMastery.com to download worksheet #7 on positioning your book for success.

Let me be candid: my true hope is that you'll see past the narrative of this book and focus on the educational value instead. I would love for you to implement the same lessons I've learned and accelerate your own journey. You probably know other people who might be struggling themselves. Please tell them about this book. Inevitably, that is how books succeed. Regardless of the marketing campaign behind them, its word-of-mouth marketing that drives a book's success.

The sad reality is that many average books make it to the bestseller list as a result of expensive marketing programs, while many *incredible* books never sell more than 5,000 copies! It's a pay-to-play world. Those with deep pockets can buy exposure and buzz, while those with limited funds rarely get noticed. The exception is when a true gem is released and people start telling their friends about it. The first Harry Potter book is a great example of this, as is *The Alchemist* by Paulo Coelho.

I've secretly had *The Alchemist* in my mind as a model for this book from the very start. It's a fictional book about a boy on a journey to find his purpose. It's a story, but it's also full of inspirational lessons. Any businessperson should read that book. Anyone with ambitious goals should read it. Anyone who is searching for his or her purpose should read it. And what happened when the book was released? People told their friends, and their friends told other friends, and the book became a huge bestseller.

I'm not suggesting this book is in the same league as *The Alchemist* but my hope for it is the same. My journey has taken me to every corner of the globe, and I've learned some incredible lessons along the way. This is a story about someone who started out with no credentials at all and who made it anyway. There were never any homeruns. There was never any big budget marketing campaign. It was just a step-by-step journey that eventually led to success. That's a story that needs to be heard by people who are building their own careers and making an impact on the world.

For me, the *process* has become the credential, and that's true for any profession. Once you start *doing* the things that leaders in your industry are doing, you start to *become* one of those leaders yourself. The road to *being* is through *doing*. That's what this book is about. It's about holding your breath and taking the plunge. It's about having faith and doing the *big* thing rather than the average thing. It's about coming down on your goals from above.

STRUCTURE OF A KEYNOTE

I write my speeches as if they were songs. I don't follow this structure every time, but it's helped me a ton over the years so I thought I'd share it with you. Think about a song. It has verses and it has a chorus. Usually, it also has what I refer to as a *bridge,* which you can think of as the guitar solo. Guitar solos were more common back in the 80s, but even today, songs generally have a climax where the pattern of the song changes and the intensity goes up.

Every speech needs a primary message, and it can be as little as three words. During his 2008 presidential campaign, Barack Obama used "Yes we can" for his message. He came back to that short phrase multiple times during his speech, ensuring his audience remembered that primary message long after his speech was over. That primary message is the chorus of the song. You come back to it over and over again, throughout the song.

Your speech also needs a series of arguments and those are the verses. Each argument should support your primary message. Also, each argument should last eight to 10 minutes. Ideally, it will include a message of its own and a story to demonstrate the point. Stories sell. Whenever possible, include stories in your speeches because people remember stories, especially when they include emotional situations they can empathize with.

My standard speech format is:

1. Introduction
2. Chorus
3. Verse #1
4. Chorus
5. Verse #2
6. Chorus
7. Verse #3
8. Chorus
9. Bridge
10. Chorus
11. Conclusion

The number of verses you have depends on the length of time you have for the speech. Your introduction will probably last three or four minutes, and your conclusion will last another two or three. For now, let's assume your bridge lasts four minutes as well. For an hour-long speech, that leaves about 50 minutes for the verses and choruses. If your average verse is nine minutes and the chorus adds one more, you have time for five main points. If you decide to use longer stories, you may elect to make just three main points and have each one last about 16 minutes.

It's very important to *not* go over time. This is a major pet peeve for meeting and event planners. If one session goes over, it backs up the entire day. If multiple sessions go over, it eats up the networking time in between the last session and the dinner. Keep in mind that the networking is the most valuable part of a conference and as a result, for the event planner as well. As a professional keynote speaker, the best thing you can do is to always finish five minutes early. Believe me; nobody will ever complain.

I once spoke at an HR conference in Nashville. The vast majority of my speaking sessions are scheduled for 60 minutes and this one was no exception. I had a good presentation ready, but it went by much quicker than I expected. I was done in 40 minutes. That was too short and I felt badly about it. Nobody complained and I had nice feedback from some of the attendees, but I knew I screwed up. Practice your speeches and try to shoot for 52 to 57 minutes for a 60-minute session.

It's also important to meet the audience where they are. Let me explain that. Audiences vary widely. Some are extremely energetic while others are more subdued. If you ever speak at a multi-level marketing event, the room is sure to be bursting with energy. On the other hand, if you speak in Sweden or Finland, it will be quiet. There's nothing worse than having a speaker come on stage and start jumping around and pumping his fists in the air in front of a quiet audience. Don't do that. When you begin your speech, try to match the energy of the room. If they're excited, you can be excited as well. But if they're quiet, start off quiet yourself.

The purpose of the first three or four verses is to build trust with your audience, guide their thinking towards your primary message and nurture their energy from wherever they started to a higher level. Start casually and subdued, but then start building the energy as you go along. The audience won't even notice that the level of energy is changing, but it will make a big difference in the end. You want the energy to reach its peak just before you finish.

Each argument should pave the way for the bridge. So what's the bridge? It's the "surprising truth." In order to generate buzz at your events, you have to challenge a conventionally held belief. You have to introduce something that's a bit of a surprise for attendees. I call it the surprising truth. Ideally, it's something where most everyone thinks one way, and you make the case for an entirely different perspective.

The place to introduce it is during the bridge. It's near the end of the speech and you've been making the case for this surprising truth right from the very first word. Your arguments should've already brought the audience in this direction so by the time you say it, it shouldn't seem so surprising anymore. It should seem logical at this point. It should seem reasonable but nevertheless, very different from what they were thinking before.

Visit **KeynoteMastery**.com to download worksheet #8 on the structure of a keynote speech.

In my social media presentation, my surprising truth is that there's been a wholesale shift in the way we evaluate content. I described this back in the Social Media Victories section. Today, people evaluate the content *first* and only see who created the content second. That's a thought-provoking idea. It gets people thinking. It's not that they believed the opposite before but for most, it's an unexpected implication that they hadn't considered yet.

The surprising truth is the highlight of your speech. I like to raise my voice a little and use a somewhat stern tonality. I want to be passionate about the message and really try to drill it into them. People engage with passion. It's the most passionate politicians who win elections. It's the most passionate entrepreneurs who get the financing and inspire action from their employees and customers. It's the most passionate musicians who capture the imagination of their fans.

Remember the musician Prince? Or perhaps I should say "the artist formerly known as Prince." He was well known for getting incredibly passionate in his songs. His bridge was rarely a guitar solo. Instead, it was *him* yelling and screaming about the subject of his song, usually a woman. I love listening to his song called "The Beautiful Ones" where he basically goes crazy near the end of the song, screaming his love for the girl. It's a perfect model for a speech.

It's obviously not realistic to literally yell and scream at your audiences, but it's sometimes surprising how close you can get to that. As long as you've built the energy up along at a steady pace, you can indeed end up with a huge amount of passion and energy by the time you get to your bridge. And just like Prince fans, audiences love watching speakers get passionate about their topic. I recorded a video about this speech structure and you can find it here:

http://www.keynotemastery.com/structure/

41

THE LAW OF STATE TRANSFER

There's a concept in social-dynamics theory called "The Law of State Transfer" which basically suggests that your emotional state will tend to transfer to the person you're speaking with. This is an invaluable concept in sales training. If you want your prospect to be excited about the product, you need to be excited about it first. If you want them to trust your advice, you need to trust your *own* advice and speak with confidence and conviction. If you're insecure, they'll be insecure. If you're confused, they'll be confused. Whatever you're feeling, the person you're speaking with will likely start feeling the same thing.

As human beings, we're hardwired for this. Even babies just a few days old can already tell the difference between a smiling face and a frowning face. And at just seven months, they use your facial expressions as social cues for how they should be acting themselves. We don't even realize we're doing this. It all happens subconsciously. We unknowingly read thousands of subtle cues including voice tonality, body posture, facial expression and even pupil dilation to evaluate a person's emotional state and then mirror that same state ourselves.

This relates to the visiting diplomat metaphor. When you act that way, you're treating yourself as if you're important and as a result, other people treat you that way as well. As the speaker, you are indeed someone important, at least at that particular event, and you have to treat yourself with respect before you can expect anyone else to do so.

When you're on the stage, it's exactly the same way. If you want the audience to find something funny, you have to see the humor in it yourself. If you want the audience to get emotional about something, you have to get emotional about it first. And if you want the audience to get excited, you have to get excited first. That's where the passion comes in. If you're passionate about your surprising truth, your audience will see the significance of it at the same time. They'll understand that this is something important, and they'll consider it more than they would if you said it without any passion or excitement.

The ideal outcome for an event planner is for your speaking session to end with a lot of excitement and buzz left in the room. One of the primary objectives of all event planners is to get the attendees to talk to each other. You want to build interactions between attendees. That's what buzz is. It's when people are enthusiastically speaking with each other and discussing ideas. That's the ultimate measure of successful networking events and in the end, all conferences are just glorified networking events.

The surprising truth is the key to generating buzz. You make the argument throughout the speech, building energy along the way and then hit them with an insightful and thought-provoking surprising truth right near the end. As soon as you finish explaining that surprising truth, you repeat your primary message one more time (the chorus) and conclude. Boom! The speech is over and everyone's fascinated with the implications. They immediately start speaking with each other and discussing the topic amongst themselves, and the event planner is thrilled.

MAKE IT FUNNY!

I spoke at a conference in Arkansas once and arrived during the afternoon of the first day of the conference. My session was on the second day. Anyway, the whole place was buzzing because of the lunchtime keynote. Of course, I was immediately curious what he did that was so awesome. Turns out, it wasn't fascinating or insightful at all. In fact, most of the people I asked could hardly even remember what his primary points were. So why were they all raving about it? He was funny.

Humor is incredibly valuable. Some people have a very natural and clever sense of humor, and I'm admittedly jealous of that. Actually, Josh has that. Ever since I first met him in Toastmasters in 2006, I've been amazed at his jokes and quips. He has a gift for it, and I wish I had it myself. If you can make someone laugh, it immediately draws them closer to you. People can't help but like you if you make them laugh. It's an enormous gift.

There's a saying that "people learn when they laugh" and it's very true. In the case of that lunchtime speaker, it didn't matter because it didn't seem like he had much real content anyway. But for someone who has valuable insights to give, the audience will learn more if they laughed along the way. The reason is that laughter short-circuits the natural human instinct to judge. When you're laughing, you stop judging the messenger (the speaker) and focus on the message instead.

I truly believe that I could double or even triple my business if I was funnier. Once, I posted a job on the outsourcing platform, oDesk.com (now UpWork.com), for a humor writer or comedic writer to add jokes to one of my speeches. I had the whole speech already written out, more than 9,000 words in total. I ended up hiring two different guys, one in Texas and the other in New York, and paid them each $100 to make my speech funny. Within a few days, I had the transcripts back with two different sets of jokes included. Honestly, there were a bunch of jokes I really couldn't use, but they both had a couple of lines that I ended up incorporating into the program, and all for just $200. Money well spent.

Humor has a lot to do with confidence and comfort. If you're comfortable in a given situation, it's easier to see the humor in things. When you're nervous, the jokes just don't come. Of course, if you're already funny, that's awesome. Seriously, you have a huge advantage as a speaker if you're funny. But if you're like me, focus on your confidence and comfort and then trust that the laugh lines will emerge.

The funniest program I ever delivered was in San Diego. It was for the California Insurance Wholesalers Association (CIWA) and I had the place in stitches. It actually surprised me as much as anyone else, but there were a number of factors that contributed to it. For starters, I had spoken at a string of events in the insurance industry and was extremely comfortable in front of those audiences, but there was another factor that played an important role.

Empty space kills events. I'm talking about the seating arrangement. People are far more likely to laugh if they're seated close to other people. When people are spaced out, they're much more conscious of the noises they make, and they're far less likely to laugh as a result. Theater-style seating is the best because the chairs are very close to each other. Meanwhile, round-circle tables are the worst because the people are spread out too much.

The room in San Diego was set up theater style and almost every seat was taken. Better still, there were two guys in that room who both had loud, funny-sounding laughs. So if either of them started laughing at something, other people would laugh just because of the way they sounded. And if they *both* started laughing, the whole room would erupt.

When the session was done and everyone cleared out, the event planner said she had never heard that group laugh so much. I felt like a god. I'm not a naturally funny guy, so it was a foreign feeling for me, but a very good one. And then, at the dinner that evening, the emcee referenced funny lines from my session twice and got me to stand and raise my hand so everyone could see where I was sitting. It was unreal.

Like I said, I truly believe I could double or triple my business if I was funnier, and you should think about your own instincts with humor and how you can use them to your advantage. Whether you're a professional speaker or a business owner or a manager with a team at work, humor can be an invaluable tool for building trust and affection from those you work with.

STEPHANIE

I still did a lot of free gigs in 2011 (28 to be exact) and a number of them were for consulting audiences. I spoke for the Bay Area Consultants Network (BACN) in San Rafael and that led to three events for the Consultants Network of Silicon Valley (CNSV) in San Jose, an event for the Bay Area Biomedical Consultants Network (BABCN) in San Mateo and two events for the Institute for Management Consultants (IMC) in Emeryville and Sacramento, respectively.

It was at the IMC event in Sacramento where I met Stephanie Chandler. She was the organizer of the Sacramento Speakers Network and asked if I would be interested in speaking at one of their upcoming meetings. It was another free event, and I was initially reluctant but was curious about the group and agreed to come in June.

The event was held at the Doubletree Hotel and the room was crammed with 54 people in attendance. Apparently, they usually had their meetings in a larger room downstairs but it was being used for another event, so we were moved to this smaller alternative. Stephanie opened the meeting and invited everyone to make a 30-second introduction before my presentation.

I listened to the introductions with fascination. Everyone in the room was trying to develop their speaking careers, either as a standalone profession or as a marketing channel for their other services. It was amazing to sit amongst these people who were all pursuing the same career that I was building myself. I felt tremendous empathy for the process they were all in. Of course, they mostly presented themselves as successful speakers, but I could immediately sense the struggle behind their words.

I had my usual Social Media Victories presentation ready to go but wanted to address the elephant in the room first. I wanted to tell these people that I was trying to become a speaker too and that the journey was long and hard, but also incredibly rewarding and exciting. I wanted to tell them about Sweden and Aruba and India. I wanted to tell them about Bloomberg. I wanted to tell them about the free circuit, the cheap circuit and the pro circuit.

The introductions finished up and Stephanie introduced me to the group. Right off the bat, I told them that their introductions touched me and that I really understood the journey many of them were on. I told them that I had spoken at 72 events in 2008 and only got paid for two, 127 events in 2009 and got paid for six, 64 in 2010 and got paid for 21 and that I was doing even better so far in 2011. I didn't spend a lot of time on it, but reassured them that progress does happen over time and the resulting pro-circuit gigs were well worth the struggle. After that, I dove right into my presentation.

My conversion rate for book sales was extremely consistent back then. 30% of attendees would buy my book. On every important PowerPoint slide, I added a little graphic of the book in the top-right corner with a reference to the chapter where that topic was discussed in more detail. During my presentation, attendees would see that little book graphic a total of 18 times, each one acting as a subtle suggestion that they should buy a copy. It was a brilliant addition to my presentation and resulted in an amazingly consistent sales ratio. Best of all, I never had to pitch my book at all. I just focused on delivering value and explaining my case histories and the sales would happen all on their own.

Thirty percent of 54 is 16. If it was a good night, I might sell 17 or 18. I actually sold 36 books that night! That's a 66% conversion rate, the highest I have ever had. The response was extremely positive. Of course, the fact that the room was so tightly packed played a part. Remember, empty space kills events. There was very little empty space that night. But it was also the little pep talk at the beginning. The attendees loved it. They felt understood, and I felt like I was among friends. We were all in the same struggle, and they really wanted to learn from my experiences.

Stephanie also ran a local mastermind group. If you're unfamiliar with that term, it's when a group of people gets together and takes turns brainstorming solutions to their respective problems. Each member gets a 20 or 30-minute "spotlight" and they can use it to discuss any issue or topic they like. The role of the other members is to then brainstorm ideas, tools or strategies to solve their problem. Masterminding is well known to be an effective medium where business owners can discuss their challenges and develop strategies for success.

When Stephanie asked me if I'd like to join, I was hesitant. I've known for many years that I don't really play well with others. I don't do well with supervision and generally don't like sharing my struggle with others. I don't like failing in public. My career has included so many failures that I instinctively want to trudge through the mud in private. Let's face it; that's why I'm self-employed. I had good jobs in my earlier life, but the supervision paralyzed me. I hated it. In the end, I just wanted to be left alone.

I also knew, however, that my solitary lifestyle was holding me back in other ways. I was still single, after all, and needed to learn to socialize with others for that reason alone. I also wanted to learn from other self-employed people whom I had respect for. Stephanie definitely seemed like someone I could respect and learn from, and perhaps her mastermind group included others of a similar caliber. She said I could visit the group once as a guest and that would allow me and the other members to evaluate each other. I agreed.

I ended up joining that group in September of 2011 and am very happy I did. It's a group of very smart people—people who were 100% responsible for their own income, just like me. I've been a member ever since and have recently used my spotlights to discuss the upcoming launch of this book. I've learned a tremendous amount from that group and remain grateful to have met Stephanie at that IMC event.

The Sacramento Speakers Network event also led to two events with the uLink Network, a business-networking group in the Sacramento area. The co-founder of that group was Jim Pelley, a professional speaker himself. In fact, Jim had apparently spoken in Dubai on three different occasions and had made a lot of money in the process. I spoke with him once and heard about his experience over there. He reminded me of Craig Valentine from Toastmasters. I was still determined to speak in Dubai myself one day.

Stephanie's also a great example of thinking bigger and coming down onto your goals from above. She's the founder of Authority Publishing, the company that published this book, but she also founded the Nonfiction Writers Conference and the Nonfiction Authors Association. The association even grants awards to non-fiction authors. Imagine the positioning! Did she have any competition? Nope! Nobody thought to do that before. By thinking bigger and stepping into that leadership role, she's put herself in the middle of a thriving community of authors and experts.

THE $10,000 DAY

My speaking engagements at insurance conferences brought me my first $10,000 day. I had already spoken at about a dozen insurance conferences and ended up speaking at the exclusive APPEX Insurance Summit in Chicago. The hosting company was called Marshberry, and they sold management consulting, merger and acquisition services to the CEOs and owners of independent insurance brokerages. The audience was full of very successful and wealthy people.

My first session at APPEX was in the fall of 2010, and they asked me to come back again for the spring conference in May 2011. While there, I met a regional VP for United Healthcare in Minneapolis and she asked if I was available three weeks later for their executive forum. That event catered to a similarly affluent and successful group, and she thought my social media session would be perfect for them. I was available and we negotiated the fee on the spot.

Credit Card Balance: $14,419 (May, 2011)

That event in Minneapolis was the one where Condoleezza Rice spoke. As a reminder, I was paid $6,000 for the event and she was paid $150,000! It was funny because they had a number of speakers but had only purchased books from two: Condoleezza and myself. They had a large table set up with piles of those two books, stacked right beside each other. In retrospect, I should've taken a picture! Anyway, I spoke on Tuesday and she spoke on Thursday so I never even met her.

My session had only 60 people in it but they were all CEOs and owners of independent insurance brokerages. The session went very well, as usual, and one of the executives from United Healthcare approached me after and said they could use my help developing their own corporate social-media marketing plan. Hmmm. "Help" probably meant consulting and that was something I had no experience doing. Nevertheless, we exchanged cards and agreed to follow up after the meeting.

I was very nervous about the conference call we scheduled. Not only was I unsure of myself in a consulting capacity but I also had no idea what to charge. Nevertheless, I was confident discussing the topic. I had delivered my Social Media Victories keynote at least 200 times at that point and was comfortable breaking down the social media conundrum into a structured implementation plan. Everyone on the call seemed excited about the possibilities.

Eventually, they asked me what my fee was. This was one of those situations where I had no idea if the number I was about to blurt out was even reasonable, but I held my breath and dropped the bomb. "I don't normally do consulting, so I really don't know what they charge. But as a keynote speaker, I usually get paid $10,000 plus travel, so I guess I would charge that," I said casually.

The hardest part of saying something like that is keeping silent after the words have come out of your mouth. I've been in that situation a few times before, and that silent period always feels like it lasts forever, and this was no exception. I stayed silent and eventually, the executive said, "Okay, that's fine. We'll get back to you." Had I just lost the job? I had no idea. We exchanged a few pleasantries and ended the call, and I sat on my couch wondering what had just happened. The uncertainty didn't last long. I received an email from him the next morning, suggesting possible dates for me to fly out.

I spent hours preparing for this trip. I spoke with friends who had experience with consulting. I pulled out a workbook I once took from one of Jeff & Kane's weekend workshops. I even searched online for management consulting advice. I would be meeting with about a dozen senior marketing executives of one of the largest health insurance companies in the country. It was an intimidating proposition.

Credit Card Balance: $18,308 (September, 2011)

I remember the morning of my full-day session. I had taken an Ativan the night before, gotten some sleep and was having breakfast in the hotel restaurant. I added some ketchup to the scrambled eggs on my plate and was using my knife to cut through a piece of bacon. It was cooked crispy and the knife wasn't cutting through it easily, so I applied a bit more pressure.

All of a sudden, the bacon snapped in two and my knife slid across the plate and catapulted a piece of scrambled egg into the air. It had ketchup on one side. Everything went into slow motion and I watched the egg rotate in the air as it approached my white shirt. I was terrified as it got closer and closer. By the grace of God, it bounced off my shirt without the ketchup even touching my shirt and the mark left behind was hardly even visible.

These are the gifts you receive from time to time. Sometimes, you just get lucky. Yes, I know it wasn't a big deal, but it would've been very frustrating for me if I ended up with a ketchup stain on my white shirt. For someone making $10,000 for one day's work, it would've been embarrassing to say the least. And here I am, years later, still remembering it as if it was yesterday.

The day went well. My friends' coaching was extremely valuable. I used a flip chart and got their input along the way. There were three different points where I encouraged group brainstorming. There were eight people in the room and another six on a conference call with a speakerphone in the middle of the conference table. Everyone participated and we ended up with some great campaign ideas. One of the attendees even told the primary executive that he should take me out for a good steak dinner that evening!

We did, in fact, go out for steak that night. He took me to the best steakhouse in Minneapolis with a beautiful view of one of their many lakes. Over dinner, he told me that he was really happy with the day, but he also said "But we have to talk about your rate." I guess I wasn't surprised. Going forward, we agreed that $500 per hour was more reasonable. Boo, hoo! Only $500 per hour ... how will I survive? High-class problems.

Every keynote program you develop needs to have a more in-depth consulting equivalent. I have left tens of thousands of dollars on the table because I didn't have consulting options available back then. I still have work to do to solidify my consulting offerings but I'm working hard at it and recommend you do the same.

I flew home the next day and looked around at all the people sitting around me in the economy section. Had any of these people made $10,000 in a single day? Of course, I spent at least three full days preparing for the session and also spent one day flying out to Minneapolis and another day flying back, but even still. I felt like I had graduated to another level in my career. Little did I realize it would take me another two years before I earned that daily rate again.

GOING INTERNATIONAL

I discovered outsourcing in 2010. Websites like Elance.com and oDesk.com (now UpWork.com) allow people to post jobs and have applicants from all over the world apply. Many of the applicants are happy with $2.00 or $3.00 per hour. I heard about these websites originally in the Entrepreneur & Small Business Academy. The successful people seemed to be hiring help in places like India and the Philippines.

I posted a job for a Virtual Assistant and had dozens of people apply for the job. It wasn't full time. I was expecting between 10 and 20 hours each week. Eventually, I hired Uma in India for $2.50 per hour and started getting her help on a variety of projects I had been dreaming about. I had her respond to "call for speakers" announcements when they were posted online, write content for my website and research and compile lists of event planners around the world.

Remember the HR conference I spoke at in Toronto? The one with the blizzard the night before? I got that gig from Uma's efforts. They issued a call for speakers on their website and Uma filled in the form. They responded and the negotiations started from there. A few months later, I found myself in the snow!

The list of international event planners was a project that evolved from my success in Sweden in 2007 and the other countries I had spoken in since then. Those international events were building my credibility back home and I wanted more, so I asked Uma to do research online and find contact names for people who worked at event-planning companies, convention & visitors bureaus (CVBs) and destination management companies(DMCs) in major cities around the world. Uma eventually completed a list of 68 names along with mailing addresses and phone numbers, and I sent each person a package with a cover letter and a printed speaker one-sheet.

A friend of mine was a graphic designer and did an awesome job designing a fancy 17" x 11" glossy one-sheet that was folded down the middle, creating a full-color, fold-out 8½" x 11" promotional flyer. I also ordered custom envelopes with my picture and website address printed across the front. Once compiled, they were professional-looking packages and I was proud to send them out. The project cost me a small fortune, but I was determined to develop my business internationally. I sent those packages out in March 2011.

I didn't hear anything back from the mailing. Like so many other experiments over the years, it seemed like another failed marketing experiment. When you're self-employed, you always have to spend money *first* and only then find out if it yields any results. I always picture myself standing on the edge of a cliff with a stack of hard-earned cash in my hand. I then have to throw the money over the edge and hope that the wind blows it back to me. Most of the time, it doesn't and the cash is gone forever. In some cases, it blows back a few dollars but rarely the original amount. This one didn't seem to blow back any bills at all.

Credit Card Balance: $17,618 (August, 2011)

In August 2011, five months later, I received an email from Ali Al Kamali. I thought it was a joke at first. Is that a real name? He lived in Dubai and was one of the people Uma identified from her research. He was interested in having me speak at a conference in

2012. I was obviously excited but I also thought the odds of this thing happening were probably less than 5%. As you might have guessed by now, this was the connection that led to my first trip to Dubai in May, 2012, which I described in detail at the beginning of this book. It was a trip that literally changed my life.

It was clear from the email string that my value was defined by the fact that I was an American from Silicon Valley. It was just like the IMC Conference in Stockholm, Sweden, in 2007. Ali Al Kamali was the founder of a company called Datamatix and they hosted a number of conferences each year including the annual GCC eGovernment & eServices Conference. It was an annual conference in Dubai and this was their 18th year.

Just like Sweden, there were times when I thought the opportunity was dead, but I kept emailing and basically pestered Ali to death. I sent him videos and references. I looked into flights and sent possible itineraries. I did whatever I could to stay in touch with him and move the process forward. The conference wasn't until May 2012, but I wanted to secure the opportunity more than anything.

I kept thinking about Craig Valentine from the Toastmasters Speech Contest in 2008 and Jim Pelley from the uLink Network in Sacramento. I had only met Jim a month before Ali's initial email in August and could still remember the conversation I had with him on the phone. This was my chance. This was my chance to rise to their level.

This opportunity was similar to Sweden in other ways too. Like Lennart Svanberg, Ali wasn't prepared to pay me anything to attend. He offered to pay for my travel expenses but nothing more. I was disappointed but it didn't diminish my enthusiasm at all. This was another one of those opportunities that I absolutely *had* to secure. If I could find a way to pull this off, I would *become* the guy who spoke in Dubai. The road to *being* is through *doing*. I needed this credential.

Credit Card Balance: $10,651 (May, 2012)

Eventually, the trip did come to pass. It was held at the Ritz-Carlton Hotel in downtown Dubai and I stayed at the Millennium Plaza Hotel across the street for six nights. I was treated like royalty while there and thanks to Boyd, the other speaker from Amsterdam, was able to explore the city more than I ever imagined possible. The hotel had an extravagant breakfast buffet each morning and I remember sitting by the window eating omelets and croissants while looking through the window at the Burj Khalifa shimmering in the morning sun. I didn't make any money, but it was the best investment I could imagine. You can find a video and a few photos from that trip here:

http://www.keynotemastery.com/dubai/

When I got back home, I created a map on Google Maps and put little blue markers on all the cities I had spoken in. My goal was to demonstrate visually that I was an international speaker. It was already quite impressive. I had markers in Sweden, Finland, Portugal, India, Dubai, Mexico, Aruba, the Cayman Islands, Canada and dozens of cities across the United States. I featured that graphic prominently on my website.

Those blue markers became my primary focus. It was a tremendous marketing tool. It established instant credibility. As soon as people saw it, they understood that I had literally traveled the globe as a keynote speaker. I wanted markers everywhere. I fantasized about filling up that map. I thought about cities in Asia, Australia and South America. I thought about Moscow and Cape Town. I imagined events in Bahrain and Riyadh. The map was a way for me to clarify and visualize my goals.

The objective was to add *permanence* to the trip. When I spoke in Sweden, I added it to my biography. That made it permanent. I

179

later added Finland, Canada and India, but my bio couldn't mention an ever-expanding list of cities. It wasn't realistic. I needed another way to communicate my experience at international events. The map was perfect. By adding those little blue markers, it immortalized each event and communicated my accumulated international experience in seconds.

> Add permanence to everything you do. Find a way to incorporate evidence of your achievements in your marketing presence. If you've spoken for a series of Fortune 500 firms, add their logos to your website. If you've been featured by well-known media outlets, add those logos as well. I've done both on my own website along with the map, and it's made a huge difference in my business. It establishes credibility immediately.

It's also interesting to see how it affects my inquiries. Once I add a marker from a particular region of the world, I start getting more inquiries from that same region. It makes sense. People who find my website are reassured when they see that I've been to their neck of the woods, and it increases the odds that they'll contact me about their event. It reduces the risk for prospective clients.

Visit **Keynote**Mastery.com to download worksheet #9 on adding permanence to everything you do.

46

THE UK CHURCH SCAM

I was at San Francisco International Airport (SFO), waiting for my flight to Dubai, when the email came in. I read it on my phone. It was from Reverend Michael Silver from the Emmanuel Evangelical Baptist Chapel in Newport, United Kingdom, and he invited me to speak at their Leadership Development Workshop at the beginning of June. It was less than one month away and I replied to his email as soon as I got to my hotel in Dubai.

I casually mentioned that I was speaking in the Middle East and quoted my speaking fee as $10,000. They agreed. The saying "it's too good to be true" doesn't apply in the speaking business. I was in a luxury hotel in Dubai. I had experienced opulence and grandeur in cities around the world. There were many things in my career that were too good to be true but they actually *were* true, so this opportunity in England didn't strike me as suspicious. It just seemed like another crazy opportunity, that's all.

With only three weeks before the trip, they were quick to provide hotel reservations, ground transportation confirmations and details on the Tier 5 Work Permit that I would need to enter the country. I researched the Tier 5 Work Permit online and it did appear necessary in certain circumstances. The standard processing would take at least four weeks but there was apparently a lady in the parish, Patricia Coleman, who worked for the UK Border Agency and she could manually expedite the process.

The form they sent to me was the same as the form on the Border Agency website. Everything seemed well organized. There was no reason for me to question what was going on. In fact, the preparations seemed significantly more organized than my experiences with past events. Keep in mind that I was in Dubai while this process was unfolding. Within that context, everything seemed fairly normal.

I completed the form and sent it to Patricia and she told me that I would have to send her the application fee via Western Union so she could submit the application on my behalf. I didn't like the idea, but the fee she quoted matched the expedited fee referenced on the website and I felt compelled to trust the process. I sent the money. Yup, I sent the money. Ugh. After all the Western Union fees, it worked out to about $900 and I, of course, never saw that money again.

I was still hopeful until they emailed me again two days later and requested another 2,500 GBP for a "bond" to enact my stay. That's when the music stopped. I knew it was a scam. I know I should've seen it coming, but the level of detail they were providing was unrivaled. I was communicating with five different people. All of the arrangements seemed legitimate and well organized. Honestly, they did a great job with the execution, and they swindled me out of $900.

After the dust had settled, I wrote a detailed blog post about the experience and it's now the second-highest trafficked post on my website. This scam is alive and well, and my post receives spurts of traffic as these scammers send out new solicitations. One day, Stephen Baldwin called me (Alec Baldwin's brother) from the airport in New Delhi, India! He had been solicited by the same people and was researching the opportunity before responding.

I contacted the police and the FBI. I contacted the equivalent organizations in the United Kingdom. Because of the international nature of the scam, nobody wants to take ownership of the problem. These scams are rampant and almost impossible to investigate. The blog post was my best revenge.

Don't ever send money to anyone! If you get an inquiry from a church, check their website for corroborating information. Be suspicious of email addresses from public providers like Gmail, Hotmail or Yahoo! Search for their email addresses on Google. I've had hundreds of comments on my blog post and many of them include the contact details of other similar inquiries. A simple Google search for the email address will immediately bring you to scam alerts like the one on my own website.

47

BEING SOMEONE SPECIAL

Bloomberg hired me back again and again. I met Sandy, who was the salesperson for the Southeast United States, Tony who had the middle of the country and Scott who had the West Coast. The events were designed to build goodwill with the local cable affiliates like Comcast and Time Warner. Bloomberg would invite the local cable affiliate to host a fancy business event and they would pay for most of it. They would bring in a keynote speaker (me) and create an upscale professional atmosphere where the cable affiliate could sell cable and broadband packages to prospective business customers. In return, the cable affiliate would include Bloomberg channels in their standard cable packages.

In the speaking business, you're always labeled as the main event, but that's not true. You're never the main event. You're actually just the sideshow. The main event is whatever business objective is being pursued. In the case of Bloomberg, it's to solidify their relationships with the local cable affiliates. And for the cable affiliate, it's to sign up more business customers. Neither one has anything to do with me. I'm just the justification for the event, allowing those other business objectives to hopefully be achieved.

I remember one event in Miami. It was a scramble to get to dinner on time. My flight only landed at 5:30 PM and Sandy picked me up at the airport. I needed to take a shower before meeting up with the people from Comcast for dinner at 6:30. These Bloomberg events always have the same format. We have dinner with the big-wigs at the cable affiliate the night before the event, then get some sleep at the hotel, and eat breakfast in the morning. I'd then speak at the event and then we'd go back to the airport and fly home again.

We arrived at the hotel at 6:10 and I checked in and then managed to brush my teeth, shave, shower and get dressed in just 13 minutes, a personal record. We got back in the car and got to the restaurant at about 6:45. We were late, but it wasn't that bad. Knowing I was going to Miami, I was wearing a black suit with black shoes, a black belt and a black shirt. I looked like a pimp. It was awesome.

On the way to the restaurant, Sandy told me that we would hopefully be meeting Filemon, one of the highest-ranking executives at Comcast. Over 4,000 people, most of the southeast USA, reported up to him. She was excited about it. At the time, it didn't mean much to me. I knew he was important, but the pressure was on Sandy, not me; at least so I thought.

We walked in and the hostess brought us to the table. There were 14 people sitting already and two seats left open, both in the middle of the table, one on each side. These central seats were reserved for Sandy and me. Everybody stood up when we approached, and I immediately shook everybody's hand and did my usual visiting diplomat routine.

After brief introductions, we all sat down. I smiled broadly, laughed easily and told stories of my travels around the world. That's what they wanted to hear. As a professional speaker, you're an anomaly. People are always curious about it and want to hear what it's like. I'm good at that part and enjoy it as well. So throughout dinner, I told one story after another, much the same way as I'm doing here in this book.

Filemon was indeed at dinner. He was a tall, gracious man. He had big hands and a friendly smile. He sat right across from me and seemed to enjoy my stories as much as everyone else. Sandy sat beside him and the two of them spoke directly with each other periodically throughout dinner. It was a fancy restaurant and I had an amazing filet mignon, as did a number of others at the table. Everything seemed to go smoothly.

Sandy was elated on the ride back to the hotel. She told me how happy she was that Filemon had attended the dinner. I told her I was happy about it too, but I didn't make a big deal about it. It was at that point that she responded in a more stern tone. "You don't get it," she said. I was startled. "He only came because of you. He came because he wanted to meet the speaker."

Really? It didn't make sense to me at first, but we started talking about it and the whole picture started to clear up. By definition, the speaker is the unusual element at the event. As the speaker, you're special. You're the one at the front of the room. Everyone else earns a salary as an employee, but you travel the world and speak to groups of people at business events. It's unusual and people are naturally curious about it.

Of course, I also knew the other side of the story. I was still struggling financially. Those other people at the table probably all made more money than me. They were successful and stable in their lives. They probably all owned homes and had wives or husbands at home, and probably a few kids as well. I had none of those things. If they knew the whole story, I never would've been the center of attention, but they didn't. All they knew was that I was the speaker and I had to fill those shoes.

"Reps from other media companies would kill to have this dinner," Sandy explained. "They would kill to have dinner with Filemon. The only reason we got it is because we brought a speaker in. The only reason we got it is because you're here."

The irony was insane, but I finally started to understand the role I play as a keynote speaker. It's a crazy career. Whether you have any money or not, you need to act like a rockstar. You need to act like a celebrity. And my ongoing metaphor of the visiting diplomat was perfect. My instinct to be gracious and charming was exactly what was expected. That's what people hope for when they hire a speaker.

I have a number of things I always do. They're little details but they make a huge difference. For example, when I speak to someone at one of my events, I always start with "Hello, my name is Patrick." They already know my name. My name is posted all over the place. I've been to events where they literally had eight-foot banners with my smiling face all over them. Everybody knows my name already so when I start with that, they always do this tiny chuckle. "Yeah, I know you're Patrick," they would say, but it comes across as very humble and kind. People love it. And when your hosts see you do it, it always makes them smile. They're surprised by it, pleasantly surprised.

These little details are as important as your speech. When you're the keynote speaker, you have a role to fill. You're the visiting diplomat and it's your job to be kind and gracious. Many speakers are the opposite. This industry is known for inflated egos and arrogance. Don't be that guy or gal. Don't be a jerk. Go in with a smile on your face and kindness in your heart and everyone will be happier for it.

SOCIAL MEDIA IS DEAD

2011 was a good year for me. My revenue was over $100,000 for the first time, and I was finally able to make some progress on my credit card debts. It was amazing how differently I felt. It reminded me of January 2005. I was still in the mortgage business back then and by coincidence, had five deals close all in that one month. I made over $23,000 in one month. Financially, it was my best month ever.

It's amazing how quickly you can get used to a new reality when it is better than the one you had before. In that one month in 2005, as the money was pouring in, I felt myself relaxing from the inside out. I felt the tension drop from my shoulders. I slept better and became more spontaneous. I went out more, not necessarily spending more money but being out socially with my friends. Sometimes you don't realize how much tension you're carrying around with you until it goes away.

My financial surplus didn't last long. I hadn't made a penny in November or December and didn't end up making a penny in February or March either, so my windfall was a total aberration. This seems to be a repeating pattern in my life. Just when I think I'm turning the corner, God peeks his head out and says, "Oh, you thought you were in the clear? Yeah, sorry about that. I've got other things in mind!"

2011 was no different. It was a great year, and I was very proud of the progress I had made, but the vast majority of my revenue came from just three clients: Bloomberg, United Healthcare and BlackBerry. I made over $35,000 in November and December of 2011 and paid my credit card balance down to just $3,000, but I also saw a downturn coming. I knew I wasn't out of the woods just yet.

The United Healthcare bonanza wasn't sustainable, and the BlackBerry events were a one-time campaign by design, but it turned out there were more problems than I realized at the time. My entire speaking career was built on just one topic: social media, and the landscape was changing quickly. Facebook, Twitter, LinkedIn and YouTube were becoming ubiquitous and overhyped. Everyone had already heard two or three social media presentations by this point.

Conferences typically have "general sessions" and "breakout sessions." General sessions are the keynotes with all the attendees in one room and the breakout sessions are held concurrently in different "tracks." I've spoken at conferences with 15 tracks, meaning there were 15 different sessions taking place at the same time, although most conferences have just three or four. Attendees look at the sessions available and select the ones they're most interested in.

You can't make any money speaking in breakout sessions. Few conferences are willing to pay more than $1,000 or $2,000 for a breakout speaker and there are tons of people who are willing to speak for free. Breakout sessions are where industry vendors see opportunities to build their reputations and attract new clients. That's why they're willing to speak for free. They're at the conference anyway and view the speaking opportunity as another marketing channel.

General sessions are the prize. Even smaller conferences have budgets set aside for their general session speakers. Those are the keynotes and they need to be good, so it's easy to make $5,000+ (and sometimes much, much more) as a keynote speaker. Social media was a general session topic from 2006 to 2011, but the excitement started to fade in 2012 and it dropped from the general session category to the breakout session category, and my income disappeared as a result. In fact, my 2012 revenue was a full 40% lower than my 2011 revenue.

I didn't notice it happening at first. It just seemed like a slower year. The referrals weren't coming in the way they had during the previous two years. But as the months passed by, it became clear that I had a real problem on my hands. Not only did I lose the United Healthcare and BlackBerry business, but my topic was vanishing in front of my eyes. I needed to introduce a new topic. I needed to diversify.

Keep in mind that my trip to Dubai was in May 2012, and I was exposed to an entirely new set of topics at that conference. I covered "global megatrends" in one of my sessions and was fascinated by the research I did to prepare for it. Could I focus on megatrends? I thought long and hard about the problem. I didn't want to lose the social media topic and also needed to keep some semblance of consistency in my program menu.

Technology was one of the megatrends and social media was obviously a new technology. It was a megatrend in its own right, although few people referred to it as such. Meanwhile, other technologies discussed by other speakers at the Dubai conference were clearly reshaping the world in significant ways as well. They talked about enterprise software platforms, cloud computing and mobile networks.

I remember one speaker in particular. His name was Jorge Sebastiao, and he gave a compelling presentation about data-center architecture and how "distributed" architectures enabled new opportunities for cyber security. It may seem boring and technical, but he was a dynamic speaker and had the audience (including me) thoroughly engaged.

A decade earlier, I spent about two years building an economic forecasting model based on demographic data. It was originally inspired by *The Roaring 2000s* book by Harry Dent (1998, Simon & Schuster), but I took his basic concept and built an elaborate Excel-based model that calculated the number of people at every age in every year between 1800 and 2100. It then calculated saving and spending patterns by age, year by year, to determine the rate of increase (or decrease) over time. I spent hours working on it and was completely enthralled by its predictive potential.

During my research for Dubai, it was immediately obvious that demographics were another global megatrend. That was a significant asset as I knew the numbers well and could speak authoritatively about the shifting demographic trends in developed and emerging markets. I knew the topic. Anyway, the point is that I had a series of topics all under the megatrends umbrella and started thinking I could broaden my focus out to encompass them all.

I checked Google Trends and the keyword *megatrend* wasn't gaining much traction, so I decided to focus on "global business trends" instead. I began the process of rebranding my website and marketing collateral, but the fact was that my business was surviving almost entirely on referrals, and none of those people had global business trends in mind when they thought of me. And besides, the number of referrals was dwindling anyway, as the social media topic was fading as a keynote topic.

With Uma's help, we shifted my outbound efforts to the new topic, but it was slow going. I needed to develop my programs and accumulate entirely new content to discuss. I did enormous research that year and created literally hundreds of slides on various business trends. I focused on them obsessively, reordering the slides and adding new ones, but it just didn't have the sizzle that my Social Media Victories program had.

Bloomberg saved my year. I did six events for them in 2012, and they still seemed perfectly content with my social media program. That's $21,000. Without them, I probably would've given up. I thought about it many times, actually. I didn't want to live this way anymore. I was exhausted of the constant financial volatility and struggle. I was stressed out and my credit card balances were quickly going back up.

I felt like I needed to pull out all the stops to protect the career I had worked so hard to build, but the net result was a series of marketing experiments that weren't yielding any measurable results. Yet again, I felt like I was standing on the edge of that cliff, throwing my money over the edge. Thank God for Bloomberg! In hindsight, I realize how important that one client was to my career as a speaker.

49

TEDx SACRAMENTO

Allen Fadhen was one of the members of the mastermind group in Sacramento. He's an eccentric guy, but has done some amazing things in the past and I got along well with him. Years earlier, he wrote a book and opened a "one-book bookstore" in Minneapolis to promote it. The store was located in a shopping mall and sold just one book, his book, in 13 different departments. Every shelf featured his book, one after another, throughout the store. It was a public relations stunt and ended up getting him press coverage across the country.

Allen also developed the CARE model, which superimposed the Law of Diffusion of Innovation onto human resources and personality profiles. The Law of Diffusion of Innovation is the bell-shaped curve with early adopters at the left, the early majority beside that, the late majority after that and the laggards on the far right. The idea was that teams of employees should include people from each section because that would allow them to take an idea from inception to implementation without needing to go outside the team.

In his model, the "C" stands for creators: the people who are naturally early adopters. They're creative idea people. The "A" stands for advancers: the people who are natural promoters and like spreading the word about new ideas. The "R" stands for refiners: the people who like adding structure to new processes and creating systems to increase efficiency. And the "E" stands for executors: the people who are good at taking instructions from someone and executing the task perfectly. Allen is a 100% creator. I'm a creator/refiner.

Allen knew my struggles in 2012 and also knew about my addiction to TED talks. I had been nominated to speak at TED twice before, but nothing ever came of either one. Anyway, TED had launched the TEDx label for independently organized TED events and Sacramento was one of the first cities to host one. The curator was Brandon Weber and Allen had secured an opportunity to speak at their upcoming event in August. He offered to recommend me for the same event.

A TEDx talk could turn my career around. It could save the day. It could finally be the homerun I was waiting for. I followed Allen's instructions and recommendations to a T. He gave Brandon my name and I waited patiently for a call. Nothing. I sent him emails, but he never responded. Eventually, Allen told me that the selection committee had finalized the agenda and I didn't make the cut.

Then, a few days later, it emerged that they had elected to add an evening "salon event" on the day before the full-day program. They could fit in three more speakers, and I was given the opportunity to audition along with 49 others. It was nerve-racking and stressful but after some nail biting, they told me that I made it onto the agenda.

Attending a TEDx event is awesome but as a speaker, the most important thing you want is the video. One of the requirements to host a TEDx event is to record the speakers with multiple camera angles to create high-quality videos that can be shared online. Videos with those recognizable red TEDx letters in the background are like gold for speakers. They instantaneously give you credibility and could potentially put you in front of a huge and growing worldwide audience.

There are tons of speakers who have given TEDx talks and had their videos explode online, accumulating hundreds of thousands or even millions of views. These speakers immediately get inundated with requests to speak and can start earning significant speaking fees as a result. It was similar to becoming a World Champion Public Speaker in the Toastmasters world, but way more extreme. People like Simon Sinek, Amy Cuddy, Susan Cain and Brené Brown were immediately booked solid after their videos went viral.

I spent a good deal of time brainstorming my proposed title with Allen before getting introduced to Brandon. We needed something that sounded appropriate for a TED event. Their motto is "Ideas worth spreading" and they have a reputation for provocative and thought-provoking speakers. Allen's creative instincts were invaluable and we came up with "Learned Intuition: How to Become Superhuman." The presentation was about the instincts and intuitions you develop naturally when you're immersed in a given field.

Credit Card Balance: $16,141 (August, 2012)

The TEDx Sacramento event took place in August 2012, and my presentation went well. I couldn't wait to get the video. We were told the videos would arrive in two or three weeks but after a month, nothing had been released. Eventually, some of the other videos were released but mine wasn't among them. Two months later, nothing. Three months, nothing. Four, five, six months, nothing. I was getting more and more desperate as the days passed by. My business was on the ropes and I was holding out that this video would change the game for me. Every day, I would check my email and on YouTube, but nothing showed up.

Credit Card Balance: $19,743 (February, 2012)

I got the email in February 2013. Brandon told me that somehow, my video files had actually been lost and that I would *never* receive the video. It literally didn't exist. They couldn't find it and were giving up on the search. I was devastated. I actually cried that day. The pressure was intense. My situation was desperate. I had worked so hard and was now dying on the vine. It seemed like my dream of being a professional speaker was being torn out by force.

I did almost nothing that day. I sat on my couch for hours, trying to digest my new reality. I had been fantasizing about this video for over eight or nine months now and had watched my career basically fall apart during that time. It just didn't seem possible that it would end this way. Brandon said this had never happened before, but that there was nothing he could do. He had apparently been working hard to find a solution, but the video files had simply disappeared and he had no other options.

All my thoughts about giving up and changing careers came back. In 1994, I received my license as a financial advisor in Canada. Perhaps I should get the equivalent license here in California. I could become a financial advisor. The irony was palatable. My finances were a mess. I was 42 years old and didn't own a house and had basically zero savings. Who would take financial advice from someone like that? Yet again, I would have to play "fake it till I make it" in a brand new career. The idea turned my stomach.

I had two friends who were financial advisors for LPL Financial. I had spoken at one of their events years earlier and we had stayed in touch. I sat down with them and discussed the options. They were kind and generous and were very interested in having me join their team. I was very honest with my situation including the part about not really wanting to make the switch. They knew my back was against the wall, and I asked for their patience as I made my decision.

There was one idea that kept rolling over in my mind. I had started following a few people on YouTube. They had their own video blogs about various topics, and I was fascinated by their growing followings. Some of these guys had literally millions of subscribers and huge followings on other platforms as well. I had the right skill set to do videos like that—at least I thought I did. Perhaps I could start a video blog of my own. What would I call it? What topics would I cover?

There was one guy in particular that I wanted to model myself after. He made videos in different cities all over the world and always had famous landmarks behind him. I even recorded seven similar videos myself in the previous few months. I actually recorded the first one at the TEDx event in Sacramento. I was outside the event hall and talked about victories being cumulative. I also recorded one at an event in Orlando. Two others were recorded in my home and three more were recorded in Dubai in January. Between them, it seemed like a good start.

Credit Card Balance: $20,523 (March, 2013)

I officially launched my "Strategic Business Insights" video blog in March 2013. It was a direct result of the worst news I could imagine (that my TEDx video would never arrive), but it ended up being the best decision I ever made in my career. There's poetic justice in the chronology. I was literally at the bottom of the barrel and as a result of my desperation, started a video blog that more than doubled my business in the following few months.

As I write this, I have over 130 videos in the series and there are a number of reasons why it helped my career as much as it did. For starters, it offered prospective clients ample examples of my approach and delivery as a speaker. They can see what I look and sound like. They can also sample my content and get an idea of my prevailing message. Of course, it also shows that I'm comfortable in front of a camera and would likely be comfortable in front of audiences as well. It dramatically reduced the risk of hiring me.

It's also important to emphasize that the video blog does not add significantly to my website traffic. My YouTube channel currently gets about 90,000 views and attracts about 400 new subscribers each month, but few of them click over to my website. Instead, the videos on my site have improved the conversion rate for people who found my website through some other channel. Although it's hard to get a clear picture of attribution, I believe it has also contributed to the higher average speaker fees I receive.

The impact on my business was almost immediate. When I officially launched the series, I already had nine or ten videos and added two more each week for the first two months. So by the end of May, I had over 20 videos and noticed the conversion rate improve right way. If you're building your career as a keynote speaker or as a self-employed professional in some other field, I highly recommend video as a means of building trust with your prospects. In my experience, it works like a charm.

Keep in mind that at least 90% of people are reluctant to make videos. They don't feel comfortable in front of a camera. Perhaps they feel awkward and can't speak smoothly when the camera is rolling, or perhaps they don't like the way they look on video. Either way, they refuse to use video as a marketing channel. So if you *do* use video, you're immediately in front of 90% of your competition. I can't stress this enough. My video blog doubled my business. Consider starting one of your own.

Visit **Keynote**Mastery.com to download worksheet #10 on starting a video blog.

The funny part of this story is that Brandon Weber contacted me in May and invited me to deliver my presentation again on the day *before* the 2013 event. They couldn't allow me to speak in front of the audience again, but I could come in when they were setting up on the day before and deliver my speech to an empty auditorium. The camera crew would be there as well and they would record my presentation.

The auditorium they were using was actually much nicer and much larger than the one they used in 2012. I also had an opportunity to review my slides again and ended up doing a better job than I did at the original event. Of course, it was difficult to speak passionately to an empty auditorium but I was very grateful for the opportunity. They spliced audience clapping in afterward and uploaded the video less than two weeks after the event. You can find it here:

http://www.keynotemastery.com/tedx/

If you watch my TEDx talk, you might notice that the audience is noticeably silent during my presentation. You may also notice that the mic wire was accidentally wrapped around itself by my cheek. It's not a perfect video but I'm absolutely thrilled to have it. I added it prominently to my website and believe that it has also had a significant impact on my conversion rate. When people find my website, I look like a legitimate speaker who's serious about his career.

> There's a very clear lesson in this story. Sometimes the worst possible outcome turns out to be a blessing in disguise. In fact, challenges often turn out that way because they push us into a corner, forcing us to take action. If you're not pushed into a corner, you don't take action. But when you *do* take action, things start to happen. I was definitely pushed into a corner by the TEDx debacle, and it forced me to take action on something that dramatically impacted my business for the better.

I did an event once for a group of about 400 entrepreneurs and self-employed professionals. It was a perfect audience for me, and I described the impact of my video blog as well as my efforts to speak internationally in great detail. It was also the first time that I shared my credit card balances publicly. It was one of my most successful speeches to date and you can find it here:

http://www.keynotemastery.com/debt/

BIG DATA

I received an inquiry on December 14th, 2012, from a woman named Veena who worked for TechMahindra in India. It's a 15-billion-dollar technology conglomerate with operations all around the world. They were holding an event called Futurescapes in Dubai on January 30th, 2013, and needed a speaker to discuss "the future of IT" for their guests. They were planning to invite CIOs and CTOs from local companies and treat them like royalty for the day, hoping to secure new contracts in the process.

This was my first serious inquiry based on my new "global business trends" branding. To this day, I'm not sure how they found me, but I was both thrilled and scared to death about the opportunity. The future of IT? How was I supposed to cover that topic? This was about three months before I launched my video blog and over six months before I got my TEDx video, but they had reviewed my website and were comfortable with my approach.

Their budget was low, but it would be my second trip to Dubai and was definitely an opportunity I didn't want to miss. We agreed on $3,000 plus travel expenses and I added it to my calendar. I had five weeks to put it together and I definitely needed help.

I thought about all the people I knew who had professional familiarity with technology and simultaneously had a high-level strategic mindset. I identified seven people and arranged to meet with them all. In each case, I told them the "Future of IT" title and asked their opinion of what I should cover. It was during this process that I started to appreciate the necessary skillset of a speaker.

Remember the surprising truth? To me, it's the key to an effective speech. You have to share something thought-provoking. You have to share something that people will contemplate. But before you can *share* something like that, you have to be able to *identify* it yourself. You have to be able to look at a situation or a challenge and see the angles that are most interesting.

As children, we automatically assume that other people are fairly similar to ourselves. This continues during primary school, high school and even during our college years. But once we get out into the real world and choose our own paths, it becomes increasingly clear how different we all are from each other; at least that's how it was for me. As an adult, I'm always amazed at how different we all are.

I interviewed those seven people and only got real value from one of those conversations. It's not that the others were worthless. It's just that they didn't leave me with anything I could use. They didn't leave me with anything juicy and interesting, except one. When I described the situation to Shannon Koffman, he turned to me immediately and said, "You have to talk about Big Data. Everyone's talking about Big Data."

This was in early January 2013, and I had never heard the phrase before, but I knew immediately that it was the juicy nugget I was looking for. It reminded me of the allure of *social media* six years earlier. It was hot. It was new. It was the label that all the innovators were talking about.

I left my meeting with Shannon and started researching the topic. Google pointed me to a variety of fascinating blog posts. I did a search for only PDF files and found a few dozen worksheets and white papers. I found a playlist of 43 videos on YouTube, totaling over 6 hours of content, and watched the whole thing, taking over 20 pages of notes. The more I found, the more I started to realize the inevitability of this topic dominating IT in the years to come.

In brief, Big Data refers to the accumulation and analysis of enormous quantities of data. Governments and businesses are accumulating more and more data all the time. From mobile phones to sensors in appliances to satellites orbiting the planet to Internet analytics, the quantities of data are exploding and the promise of profitable insights is exploding as well. The biggest users of Big Data include "smart cities," telecom companies, healthcare providers, defense departments and large Internet companies like Google, Facebook and Amazon.

My presentation in Dubai combined the Big Data topic with some of my demographic work, primarily because the demographics significantly favor Africa and the Middle East in the approaching decades, and I wanted them to see that trend unfolding as clearly as the emergence of Big Data technologies. But the Big Data portion was a huge hit. It was a new term, and I described it and the underlying technologies in detail. It was music to their ears.

It was obvious to me that the Big Data program could one day replace my Social Media Victories program. I had to learn everything there was to know about the topic and accumulated more case histories to help people learn how to leverage the trend. I knew I needed a good title and description and thought about my "Monetizing Trust: Leading Your Audience from Rapport to Revenue" title back in Sweden, 2007. I decided to name my new program "Monetizing Big Data: Leveraging Predictive Analytics and Business Intelligence."

When I got home, I created two videos about Big Data for my video blog. At the time I'm writing this, one of those videos has accumulated over 150,000 views. For a business video, that's a huge number. I added the relevant keyword phrases to my website and focused on generating new content about the subject on my website. Just like my experience with social media, I was ahead of the curve and needed to establish credibility with that topic quickly.

Since that time, I've covered Big Data at events here in America as well as events in Dubai, Russia, Colombia and Oman. I've never pretended to have the technical expertise. Instead, I present myself as a strategic business analyst. My program is perfect for CEOs and executives who need to understand the trends and where the technology is being used. It's a great program for an opening keynote because it lays the foundation with definitions and case histories, and gets attendees excited about the possibilities.

This is another perfect example of the message throughout this book. I don't have the technical credentials to do what I'm doing. It doesn't matter. I don't misrepresent myself to anyone. I'm very clear and very open with what I am and what I'm not. But the reality is that the people who have the technical expertise are generally boring speakers. Meanwhile, I have the strategic perspective covered and give a dynamic and compelling presentation.

The people who book me are fully aware of the trade-off. I tell them to book me for the opening keynote and then have the technical experts come in after to dig into the software configurations and Hadoop architecture. I now have six videos on the subject so prospective clients can already see my approach to the topic, and the topic now accounts for over 30% of my income. Thank you, Shannon Koffman!

Visit **Keynote**Mastery.com to download worksheet #11 on content targeting.

BANGKOK, MOSCOW &
THE PHILIPPINES

As you might remember, July 2010 was a huge month for me: I had my first three pro-circuit gigs that month and they all went well. Three years later, I had a similar month with events in Bangkok, Moscow and the Philippines, all within 24 days. It was another scramble, and brought a whole new batch of experiences and lessons to my evolving speaking career.

Credit Card Balance: $20,815 (July, 2013)

All three of these events took place between July 16th and August 8th, 2013, and they were all very far away. As they got confirmed, it became obvious how tight the travel transfers would be. I would fly to Bangkok and came back home again, but only for three days, and would then fly to Moscow and then directly on to Manila after that. The whole thing seemed like déjà vu from three years earlier, but I was more confident this time and was ready for the challenge.

The event in Bangkok was for Capstone Financial, a financial planning company based in Australia. It was an incentive trip for their top-performing financial advisors and there were about 60 of them on the trip. I agreed to do two sessions: one about social media and a second about thinking bigger.

This second session was one of the first times I covered a "mindset" topic that wasn't built on a series of tangible case histories. I'm glad it was second because it didn't go that well. The first one, of course, went extremely well, so the group was more forgiving the second time around. I had already proven myself with the initial social media presentation. Nevertheless, I knew the second session didn't hit the mark. It wasn't bad. Nobody was upset with me, but I know how good these programs can be, and this one just didn't measure up.

My first session was right after the opening keynote, which was delivered by the Australian Ambassador to Thailand. He stayed for my session and we sat at the same table for lunch. Here again, I was secretly pinching myself. How was it possible that I would have lunch beside the Australian Ambassador to Thailand? Most people never have the opportunity to be in the same room as someone like that, much less chat over lunch together. I truly do have the best job in the world.

My second session was on the last day of the conference, and we had a river cruise scheduled for that evening. Many of these conferences take place in exotic destinations and the hosting companies regularly arrange for these types of excursions. For the attendees, they get to participate in these events once each year if they're lucky. For me, I get to enjoy them two or three times each month.

During my three days at home after Bangkok, I had a video shoot scheduled for Apollo Education Group, the parent company of the University of Phoenix. They found my Big Data videos on YouTube and wanted me to discuss the topic for an online platform they were building for job seekers. It was a professional shoot in a studio in San Francisco with makeup artists, bright lights and a ton of video equipment. I felt like a movie star, getting my makeup done for a video shoot between one trip to Bangkok and another to Moscow and Manila.

I left for Moscow the next day. Amazingly, the man who brought me to India in 2010, Rajeev Kohli, was the brother of the man who brought me to Moscow in 2013, Rohit Kohli. The Kohli brothers were both executives at Creative Travel, their family business based in New Delhi. They organized events in India for visiting travelers but also had corporate clients in India who sometimes held events in other countries. This was one such case.

The conference was for the Commercial Real Estate Development Association of India (CREDAI) and all 600 attendees were independent real estate developers: some small and struggling and others huge and successful. In this case, I had the closing keynote and spent my first three days attending other sessions. They were all given in English and I learned an enormous amount about the field.

This is one of the best parts of my job. I constantly intersect with vastly divergent industries and get to learn about different business models and different circumstances. It broadens my perspective and adds to my own content, even if only in some small way. But after dozens and dozens of different events, it's left me with an extraordinarily broad understanding of our global economy.

Similar to speaking internationally, this is another case where the process *becomes* the credential. The fact that I've spoken for so many different people in so many different industries has become an asset that I can point to for future clients. It also lessens the possibility that I'll say something stupid or naïve in my presentations. Although I still have countless things to learn, I feel like I'm sufficiently sophisticated at this point to come across as credible in most cases.

On the first day of the conference in Moscow, after brief opening remarks by the chairman of the association, the Indian Ambassador to Russia was invited onto the stage. I should've guessed! I couldn't believe it, actually. A week earlier, I had met the Australian Ambassador to Thailand and now, I was meeting the Indian Ambassador to Russia. We sat at the same table for lunch that day.

It was clear that the conference attendees were an important group. The conference was being held at the Ritz-Carlton Hotel right across Mokhovaya Street from the Kremlin and Red Square, and the ambassador was very respectful to the audience. These people controlled some of the largest construction firms in India and were building new housing units by the thousands.

On the second day of the conference, they had a river cruise on the Moskva River. No kidding. You can't make this stuff up! The Bangkok and Moscow conferences were mirroring each other in every way. The tour buses took all 600 attendees to a launching dock across the river from the impressive "Moscow City" cluster of skyscrapers, most of which were still under construction. It was a huge boat and the buffet dinner was full of Indian curries and dal. I was eating Indian food in Moscow. Go figure.

Moscow City is an area of Moscow zoned specifically for skyscrapers. Years earlier as I fantasized about traveling to famous international cities, I looked at photos of Moscow City on Google Images. It was an iconic group of buildings. Each one had a distinct architectural design. One looked like a stack of blocks, each slightly offset from the one beneath it. Another got narrower in diagonal sections, and a third twisted around as it got taller. There's a similar "twisted" building in the Dubai Marina and another in Bahrain. Anyway, I had seen this cluster of buildings on my computer screen and was now looking at them in person. My brother would've loved it.

My closing session was on the third day. The title was "Global Business Trends" and it included sections on Big Data, social media and demographics. I made a number of small adjustments to my slides, incorporating themes mentioned by other speakers during the first two days, and the session was a huge success. It was my first standing ovation, actually. They didn't all stand up, but many of them did. I was elated.

That night, Rohit Kohli took his staff out for a celebratory dinner and invited me to join them. He seemed to know where he wanted to go and told me it was at the top of one of Moscow's tallest buildings. Moscow City had the only skyscrapers in the area and sure enough, Rohit took us there. One of the only build-ings that was fully complete was the Novotel Hotel and they had a fancy restaurant on the top floor. That's where we were heading.

The taxi dropped us off in the middle of this huge construction zone. There were building materials everywhere and barbed-wire fences around the other building sites, but the Novotel Hotel was indeed open and we walked through a regal lobby to the elevator bay. When the elevator doors opened on the top floor, I was re-minded of the Atmosphere restaurant in Dubai. The ceilings were tall and the decor was beautiful. They had these enormous 20-foot windows that all opened in unison with polished hydraulicstruts. Where else would a restaurant have 20-foot tall windows that open on the 69th floor of a skyscraper?

The next day was interesting. I had to check out by noon, but my ride to the airport wasn't scheduled until 6:00 PM. I had a red-eye flight to Hong Kong that evening before transferring to a con-necting flight to Manila the following morning. I planned to just relax in the hotel lobby and work on my computer during the af-ternoon hours, but that turned out to be a bad idea.

With my overnight flight plans in mind, I was wearing very ca-sual clothes and the lobby was full of other conference attendees checking out and waiting for their rides. Many of them came up to say hello but Rohit was clearly uncomfortable with that. He didn't want me milling about with the other attendees when I was look-ing so casual. I could see it in his expression. He wanted me out of there.

Personally, I enjoy interacting with the attendees and also enjoy showing them that I'm a normal person, but that's not what Rohit wanted. He wanted me to maintain that professional image from start to finish. He wanted the visiting diplomat. It's pervasive. It's part of your role as a speaker. After about 15 minutes, he arranged for me to spend the afternoon in the Club Level on the top floor.

This was yet one more time when I found myself pinching my-self. The Ritz-Carlton was definitely fancy enough, but the Club

Level was even more extravagant. They had a lavish buffet and staff available to provide whatever you might wish for. They had vodka and caviar and a table full of desserts, all presented in fancy shot glasses just like they were in Aruba. There was a beautiful rooftop patio overlooking the Kremlin and cigar ashtrays on all the tables. The whole thing screamed of Russian opulence.

The event in the Philippines was very different. Although they had operations around the world, it was a small company and their event was taking place at the Holiday Inn in Clark, about one hour north of Manila. There were only nine people at the event, each one a vice president of a different national territory in the Asia Pacific region. One person was in charge of Singapore, another was in charge of Korea and another was in charge of Malaysia, and so on.

I did two sessions for them: the first was social media and the second was my demographic program. Predictably, the first session went well, but the second went well also. My demographic program was still in its infancy back then, but they immediately saw the implications and it sparked a lively dialog in the conference room. The CEO was extremely engaged and spoke to me after to dig deeper on the potential of demographic forecasting.

CONSULTING

This wasn't the first time someone had asked me about possible consulting, and I had deflected those opportunities almost every time. The one notable exception was United Healthcare, but even in that case, I was terrified and uncomfortable with the process. The reason is simple. I didn't have full confidence in the tactics, social media in that case, to solve the problem.

Social media is a funny thing. Much of it depends on the voice of the campaign and how it resonates with the target audience. Two different people could share virtually identical content, but one could be wildly successful while the other never gets noticed. The successful one might be funny or clever or well calibrated with the mindset of the target audience. The unsuccessful one might be awkward or inappropriate in his/her delivery.

I have always believed that as a consultant, you should have confidence that you can deliver the solution that the client is looking for. You should be able to solve the problem. Many people have told me that this is not always the case and that I am not responsible for their failures. As long as I give them good advice, I have done my job. Even still, I never felt comfortable taking money for marketing advice that might yield no results at all.

I had so much experience standing at the edge of that cliff, throwing my money over the edge and having so little of it come back. The struggle was so real for me that I felt unqualified to teach others what they should be doing. Meanwhile, despite my ongoing struggle, I had indeed built my career from nothing. I had secured speaking engagements all around the world. Those victories were all the result of my own marketing efforts on mostly digital channels.

This was the paradox I found myself in. On one hand, I was eminently aware of the potential for failure and wasted efforts. On the other hand, I had succeeded in using those same strategies to succeed in my own career. Was I qualified to teach others or not? The truth is that social media is a complete waste of time for many of the people and businesses who are using it. Yes, there are many success stories, but there are also plenty of failures.

The situation in Clark was different. I hadn't yet developed my demographic content into a concise and compelling presentation, but the core content was very good and it was 100% proprietary. I had developed it myself and as far as I knew, nobody else was exploring the same angles. The World Bank was monitoring demographic trends by country, and a bunch of financial companies were forecasting economic performance around the world, but nobody was using demographic data to forecast economic performance.

On the last day of the conference, after the last session, I shared an airport limousine with the CEO. The ride back to Manila took about 90 minutes and we talked about my research for most of that time. I didn't know how to sell consulting services, but the conversation alone was exhilarating for me, and I knew I had to develop that side of my business.

Between the two, consulting and keynote speaking, I much preferred the speaking. There simply isn't a higher-leverage option available. With keynote, I can travel to exotic destinations for three or four days, enjoy five-star amenities, speak for 60 minutes and earn $10,000 or more. With consulting, I would have to invest significant time and effort for the same payoff. Nevertheless, it would be a way for me to contribute more significantly to my clients' businesses.

I started asking my contacts about their consulting practices. I searched for "consulting proposal templates" on Google and began developing my own format. It was almost two years before I started doing more consulting, but the wheels were now in motion and I was broadening my value proposition at the same time. Every one of your keynote programs should have a corresponding consulting package. I'm continuing to refine mine and recommend you do the same.

Visit **Keynote**Mastery.com to download worksheet #12 on consulting services

SLEEPING ON PLANES

My flight home from the Philippines was booked with frequent-flyer points and the itinerary was ridiculous. I flew from Manila to Hong Kong and had a six-hour layover there. I then flew to Shanghai and had a nine-hour layover there. I then flew to Los Angeles and then up to San Francisco two hours later. All in all, it was a 30-hour trip.

As mentioned, I've never been good at sleeping on planes. My brain just won't shut down. The other problem is that I'm not comfortable sleeping while sitting in a chair. Sometimes I'll doze off for 20 or 30 minutes but never longer than that. The net result is a ton of trips where I arrive in zombie mode with that nauseous feeling of exhaustion in my stomach. I've always gotten through it, but it hasn't always been easy.

By the time I got on the flight from Shanghai to Los Angeles, it was already late in the evening for me. Remember, I had only been in Manila for four nights and was in Moscow for five nights before that, and three nights in San Francisco before that and five nights in Bangkok before that. So I was truly a global traveler by that point and my body clock had given up long ago. It didn't know when to be awake and when to be asleep. It all boiled down to the number of consecutive hours I had been awake and I was pushing 22 hours at that point.

Flights of eight hours or more all follow the same format. You get a meal shortly after takeoff and then it's lights out for the center portion. Apparently, they even change the pressure in the cabin, raising it from a 6,000-foot elevation to an 8,000-foot elevation to help the passengers relax and get some sleep. Then on the other side, they slowly turn the lights back on and serve a breakfast before you land.

When it came time to sleep, I put my tray table down and leaned forward onto it rather than leaning back in my chair. I also took my U-shaped neck pillow and placed it down on the tray table, immediately above the airplane pillow they provided for every passenger. The neck pillow allowed me to plant my head face down onto the pillow with my nose in the opening. It wasn't perfect but it allowed me to breathe normally and block out most of the distractions.

Of course, I didn't stop there. I also had my stack of supplements including glutamine, glycine and melatonin on hand. They're all supposed to help you sleep better and I took them all after the meal. And with Phyllis' advice still ringing in my ear, I added an Ativan to the mix. It added up to a perfect cocktail and for the first time in my entire life, I slept for six hours on that flight.

This was quite a milestone for me. I was on so many long-distance flights during the past few years and had never managed to get any real sleep along the way. And here I was, landing at LAX feeling alert and refreshed. It also meant the flight went by much quicker. It was a foreign feeling but one I was grateful to finally experience myself.

On three different occasions, I lost iPods because I accidentally left them in seat-back pockets on airplanes. In all cases, it was because I couldn't sleep on a long flight and was in zombie mode. In one of those cases, I actually got the iPod back again, but in the other two cases, they were gone forever. Maybe this was a new era for me. Maybe my days of losing iPods were finally over.

The whole journey, from Bangkok to Moscow and then to Manila, was a hectic three-week trip, so Josh and Phyllis met me at the airport when I arrived in San Francisco. I love the friendship we have. There's an enormous amount of empathy between the three of us, and we always help each other celebrate victories when they materialize. This was another victory and they were there to welcome me home.

We went to a sushi restaurant on the way home. I love sushi and we had some sake as well. After dinner, Phyllis felt like she had had too much to drink and Josh was really tired from a long day, so I ended up driving them home in Phyllis' car that evening. It was such a paradox. After a long flight like that, I'm usually a complete zombie. There's no way I should be driving a car. But in this case, after having slept on my flight from Shanghai, I was indeed the best suited to drive the three of us home.

MOTIVATIONAL SPEAKER

My video blog was having a major impact on my career. The videos were building trust with my website visitors and increasing my conversion rate, but that wasn't all. The video topics were also influencing the topics my website visitors were inquiring about. If I uploaded videos about a certain topic, people would eventually start asking me if I could cover that topic at their events. It made perfect sense, but surprised me at first.

My first group of videos all covered business topics. I made videos about technology topics including social media and Big Data. I made others about demographics and communication skills. They were all consistent with my existing speaking programs. But after a while, I had covered most of my standard speaking topics and started to broaden the scope. I've always been passionate about personal development and started making videos about personal development topics such as positive psychology and the science of happiness.

It wasn't long before I started getting asked to cover motivational topics at events. Also, the search volume for "motivational speaker" is 12 times higher than the search volume for "keynote speaker," so many of my website visitors were searching for a motivational speaker to begin with. That's how they found my website, and my personal development videos were a perfect fit for them.

I've never thought of myself as a motivational speaker, primarily because the field is dominated by dynamic "rah-rah" speakers like Tony Robbins. Don't get me wrong: Tony Robbins is awesome, but I'm really not that type of speaker. I mentioned this earlier in the book. I'm not into jumping up and down and doing high-fives with strangers for the sole purpose of elevating my mindset and spiking my adrenaline levels.

I do acknowledge that these strategies can be effective, but they don't fit well with my own personality and approach. I always feel stupid during exercises like that and struggle when advocating them to others. Instead, I like to appeal to people's intellect. I try to provide sound guidance based on scientific research and published studies, combined with stories of how those findings have played out in the real world.

The objective of dancing and exchanging exuberant high-fives is to create a *shift* in people's psychology. If you can get them into a higher-level state, they can see the situation from a new perspective and attach positive emotional triggers to those new thought patterns. There's good science behind this process. It's just not the approach I want to use. I prefer to present a compelling case for the new perspective and let them shift their paradigm on their own.

Having said that, I also believe strongly in the power of a positive mindset and the domino effect that results from thinking bigger. All of my videos end with the phrase "think bigger about your business, think bigger about your life," and I started getting more inquiries about that topic. I eventually developed a program called "Cultivating Greatness," which focused on positive psychology and the science of happiness.

My "Think Bigger!" session in Bangkok was my first attempt at that mindset topic. I later delivered a similar program for a franchise company based in Boston, and then again for RE/MAX in West Virginia. None of them went as well as I would've liked. Everyone was happy. Nobody complained. But again, I know how good keynote programs can be and these didn't come close. I didn't feel comfortable with the content. It wasn't tactical enough. It didn't have immediately actionable tips and tricks that I could share. And on top of that, I didn't have an inventory of good and, ideally, humorous stories that I could share.

I've given my social media program over 300 times and know it like the back of my hand. As mentioned, I'm not generally a funny guy but periodically come up with a line or two that people laugh at, and I always make note of those lines so I can repeat them at future events. Over the years, I've accumulated 15 or 20 laugh lines in my Social Media Victories program, making it as entertaining as it is educational.

I had no such laugh lines for my motivational topics and wasn't delivering the program frequently enough to hit any kind of rhythm with it. There's a very distinct feeling I get when I don't yet have confidence in a particular topic. I felt that way about the Big Data and demographic topics as well, and my only solution was to meditate on the slides and visualize the delivery over and over again. The process slowly increases my confidence in the content and the humor only comes after that point.

There are a few essential elements that characterize a good key-note speech. We've talked about the structure of the speech already, but I'd like to add a few more tips here. First, the best measure of the speech's impact is its relevance for the audience. The more relevant it is, the bigger the impact for attendees. Second, the motivational element is delivered through actionable tips and tricks. If your speech has more actionable advice, it will be more motivating. And third, the vehicle to deliver all this relevant and actionable advice is through stories. People rarely remember the facts and figures you share, but they almost always remember the stories.

There's another aspect to this. Some people suggest that the primary characteristic of great speeches is the comparison of an imperfect today with a better tomorrow. In fact, they suggest that the more times you toggle between the imperfect today and the better tomorrow, the more inspiring and motivating the speech will be for attendees.

This is why case histories are so effective in speeches. In each case, you're describing a situation of how somebody transitioned from an imperfect today to a better tomorrow. In so doing, you're toggling from the present to a better future and describing the actionable tactics that facilitated the transition. Meanwhile, the more relevant the tactics are for the people listening, the more they will get immersed into the speech. They may even enter that euphoric state where they're imagining their own better tomorrow, and you're simply narrating that journey for them.

The best speeches are those that deliver that euphoric state to attendees. You want them to be consumed by their own positive thoughts, with an increasing sense of confidence in their ability to achieve that goal. And it's during that euphoric state, built over the course of your insightful arguments (or verses) that you introduce the surprising truth, shift their perspective and solidify your message. In the end, you're delivering an empowering message for a better tomorrow.

In 2002, Stuart Kauffman introduced the concept of the "adjacent possible" which encourages thinkers to consider fresh new insights into unexplored areas. I think about this phrase when I'm building my keynote programs. I'm trying to introduce my audiences to an adjacent possible—a better tomorrow—and providing specific tactics that will get them there. If they embrace my adjacent possible and believe that my tactics are accessible and realistic, I've achieved my objective.

Visit **Keynote**Mastery.com to download worksheet #13 on maximizing your speech's impact.

This discussion could easily form the foundation of a motivational program. We're talking about shifting your mindset to create a better tomorrow. All of my research into positive psychology and the science of happiness has this same implication. I just need to figure out a format to put it all together. I've given my Cultivating

Greatness program about a dozen times now and it's slowly getting better, but still has a long way to go. So far, I've never had that same electricity and excitement with that program as I've had with Social Media Victories.

The area where it *has* worked is when I've incorporated those motivational elements into my other programs. I've created a "think bigger" closing that fits perfectly at the end of my Monetizing Big Data and Exponential Technologies programs. I've also done a more extensive think-bigger segment after having already presented another topic first. If I can get them excited with another more tactical program first, the motivational content works great as the second course. But when presented in isolation, it falls short.

I need more actionable advice and entertaining stories. In time, they will come. It takes time. People often think that you can develop a program from scratch and perfect it in preparation for a single event. That's almost impossible to do, at least for me. Instead, you deliver it again and again, making hundreds of tiny adjustments along the way, testing new content and making note of what your audience reacts to. Over months or even years, it slowly improves until you eventually have a real winner on your hands.

This is what comedians and politicians do. Comedians are constantly testing new material on their audiences. When something works, it's incorporated into the standard format. Politicians do the same thing at their campaign rallies. They test new stories and new policy statements and when they elicit a good reaction from attendees, they're incorporated into the standard stump speech.

This is precisely what happened with my Social Media Victories program. I've delivered it over 300 times at this point and it has had countless iterations along the way. At this point, it's clean and strong. Every sentence and every slide has relevance. There's a rhythm to it, a cadence. There are plenty of laugh lines and also a great surprising truth. By the end, attendees are excited and the room is buzzing. One day, I will have a similar program in the motivational category.

SPEAKING FEES

My video blog launched in March 2013, and my business started rocking a few months after that. I did a full-day workshop in Bahrain in December of that year for $15,000. April 2014 was my most profitable month so far. I earned $31,000 in speaking fees that month with $25,000 logged in just eight days. I did an event in Trinidad in July for $12,500 and another in Istanbul in October for $13,000. I booked a few more for $10,000 each here in America and one in Canada. My business bank account was flush with cash for the first time in my life and I deposited over $45,000 in after-tax earnings into my personal savings account during that year.

My standard "bureau fees" were $10,000 (plus economy travel) for North American events (including Mexico, Canada and the United States) and $15,000 (plus business-class travel) for overseas events. Without any real celebrity cachet, this is approaching the upper limit for keynote speaking fees. I've mentioned the free circuit, the cheap circuit and the pro circuit before. Well, there's a celebrity circuit at the top and that begins at about $25,000. Below that, there's an unspoken limit at $15,000 for domestic events and $20,000 for international events.

To give you one more reference point, *New York Times* bestselling authors can normally charge about $35,000 per speech, but this is specifically for *New York Times* bestsellers and not Amazon bestsellers. Marketers have long since engineered temporary sales spikes on Amazon to gain bestseller status for a few hours but that does not constitute a true bestseller. *The New York Times* monitors a variety of retail channels, both online and off, and their list is an authoritative assessment of the bestselling books at any given point in time. If your book makes the list, your speaking fee will jump up quickly.

When I first started working with speakers' bureaus, my standard fee was $5,000 plus economy travel, but I was soon told I needed to raise it. It actually came from an account executive with one bureau who called me on her cellphone and told me that at just $5,000, bureaus would rarely recommend me. They couldn't make any money. I needed to raise my fees to at least $10,000. I couldn't believe what I was hearing. To understand her perspective, let's look at the numbers.

Most bureaus take 30% of $5,000 speaking fees, 25% of fees between $5,001 and $20,000 and 20% of fees above $20,000. If my fee was $5,000, the bureau would get $1,500 (30%), but that didn't all go to the account executive. It had to be split with the company and assuming the split is 50/50 (for many bureaus, it's even less than that), the account executive would only earn $750 for booking me. When you compare that with $1,875 for a $15,000 speaker or $2,500 for a $25,000 speaker, it's no contest. They'll push the more expensive speakers every time.

There's another problem as well. When a client calls a bureau and requests speakers in a particular niche, the account executive prepares a grid with a list of about 10 possible speakers along with a short note about their respective biographies and speaking fees. The grid is always sorted by the fee so if my fee is $5,000, I'll be at the bottom of the list (or the top, depending on the sorting). Either way, I'm the cheapest option on the grid.

Within that context, it looks like there's something wrong with me. I immediately look like the newbie on the list. The lady from the bureau told me that nobody would hire me if I were the cheapest option. Even if they can only afford $5,000, they'll try to negotiate that fee with someone higher on the list. I look like the loser in the bunch. I look like the runt of the litter. I needed to be at $10,000 if I hoped to get any attention from the bureaus.

It wasn't as easy as simply raising my fees. I needed to have a website that reflected that higher fee range. I needed to raise my game across the entire marketing spectrum. That was the reason I updated my original website in October 2011. I also got my first professional demo video that same month and by early 2012, I felt comfortable officially raising my fee structure.

To be clear, raising my standard fee structure did *not* mean I started getting that fee every time. I hardly ever got that fee but with the bureaus, at least, I had supposedly put myself into contention. In 2014, I was contacted by a guy from a different bureau with almost the exact same message, encouraging me to raise my fees to $15,000 for domestic events and $20,000 for international events. To this point, I still don't feel comfortable raising my fee that high, but perhaps it will happen after this book gets released.

Visit KeynoteMastery.com to download worksheet #14 on speaking fees.

You should also know that the change never increased the amount of business I got from bureaus. In 2013, I sent postcards to all of my contacts at the various bureaus. My list included about 150 people at about 130 bureaus. The only events I have ever secured through bureaus are the Bloomberg events and the related spinoff business, with one exception. I once secured a Marriott event in Cancun through a bureau, but it was a stand-alone opportunity.

The postcard campaign generated a lot of activity. When a bureau submits your name for an event, they call or email you and request that you add a "hold" to your calendar. That way, if you get another inquiry for the same date, they get first right of refusal. You can also add a second hold and a third hold for subsequent inquiries as necessary. I got dozens of holds as a result of the postcard campaign. At one point, I had three different holds for September 9th, 2013. But even with all of this activity, I ended up securing a grand total of *zero* events. It was just another waste of money.

The evolution of the Internet is squeezing middlemen in all industries. Travel agents were among the first to go but many others have followed. Insurance agents are slowly being replaced by online platforms like esurance.com and progressive.com, and distributors and brokers across a wide variety of industries are experiencing similar pressures. The speaking business is no different. The Internet is squeezing bureaus and they're booking a smaller percentage of the total business every year. At this stage, they're still making money but in a few more years, I predict they'll start vanishing altogether.

Speakers need to aggressively develop their online presence to ensure their survival in the field. More and more corporate buyers are doing their own research online and booking speakers directly. The combination of my website and my video blog accounts for at least 70% of my new business. I believe they will become even more important in the years to come.

My average fee during 2014 was just shy of $8,000, with higher fees coming from international events and lower fees domestically. If this book does well and I find some other marketing channels that deliver better results, I believe I could eventually get to an average fee of $12,000 or $13,000. Let's assume we're talking about a speaker whose average fee is $12,000. If he/she did 50 events during a year, that would translate to $600,000 in speaking fees.

Earlier in the book, I said that $700,000 is essentially an upper limit on annual non-celebrity speaking fees. This is why I chose that number. These days, I'm doing about 30 events each year. I could do more. There are plenty of speakers who do 60 or 70 events each year but that's a lot. If each one requires travel, you're really scrambling to get from one to the next. You also have to have a thriving marketing funnel to secure that many events each year to begin with, so I think 50 events is a good number to work with.

For a non-celebrity speaker, getting an *average* speaking fee of $15,000 would be a tremendous accomplishment. If you achieved that and did 50 events each year, you'll earn $750,000 per year in revenue. The National Speaker Association (NSA) has its Million Dollar Round Table and it's a big deal for a reason. To earn over one million dollars in speaking fees, you need a powerful marketing funnel and you need to hustle.

It's worth mentioning that most members of the Million Dollar Round Table include revenue from product sales to qualify, and that's allowed. Again, it's very difficult to earn over one million dollars purely in speaking fees during a given year unless you have celebrity cachet.

If you're getting started as a speaker, I recommend you start at $5,000. At a minimum, you'll need a presentable website and a decent demo video. If you get a good TEDx video and a traditionally published book, you're probably ready for $10,000. To get past that, you need to look like a rock star. Your website needs to have some serious sizzle and you'll need significant video footage to demonstrate your stage presence. Even if you're not a celebrity, you'll need to *look* like one to get $15,000 per event.

PAID IN CASH

The second time I went to Dubai was in January 2013. That's the time I covered The Future of IT at Futurescapes for TechMahindra. My third visit was in January 2014, and the inquiry came in on a Thursday afternoon. Their event was the following week and they wanted to check my availability. The client was BMC Software and my contact was located in Singapore. They originally planned to host the event in Bangkok, but the city was plagued with social unrest and they switched it to Dubai at the last minute.

I get between 20 and 30 inquiries each month but only convert three or four into secured business. Most of them disappear—you can get an idea quickly if an inquiry is serious or not. In most cases, I reply to their inquiry and never hear back again. I've tried calling (if I have their phone number) and emailing them again and again, but when they disappear, they disappear entirely. It's very rare that they re-engage the second or third time around.

The inquiry for the Dubai event was serious and it was obvious from the start, but the communication was sparse and inconsistent and I was nervous about it. With only a week before their event, I quoted my full standard rate for international events, $15,000 plus business-class travel, but I also offered to be flexible if necessary. This is always a tricky situation. I have no idea what their budget is. If it's low, I want to offer flexibility but if it's high, I don't want to miss the opportunity to secure a significant payday.

> The trick is to offer *some* reason for your willingness to be flexible. Maybe the event is coming up quickly as in this case, or maybe they're booking far in advance. Maybe it's a city you'd love to visit or an audience that is perfect for your programs. It doesn't really matter what the reason is. You just need a reason, that's all. That way, you can quote your full rate and then offer flexibility if they're working with a tight budget.
>
> The problem is with the interpretation of the word *flexibility*. Some people may have a very limited budget and dismiss my quote immediately because the difference between my number and their number is too big. What they don't realize is that with only one week before the event, I would accept anything even remotely reasonable. As long as I get to make some money, I'm better off than I would be otherwise.

That's exactly what happened in this case. I quoted $15,000 and they disappeared. I wrote them a second email and emphasized that I will be flexible to secure the opportunity. I even referenced my trip to the Philippines, which I did for $7,000 and I paid for the flight myself. Would this be reasonable for them? I basically begged for them to respond and thankfully, they did. They offered $5,000 and I checked for flight options. I found an itinerary for about $1,100 and requested $6,100 as a counter so I could pay for the flight and earn $5,000 for myself. They agreed.

Now, here's the tricky part. Yahoo! Travel claimed there was only one more seat at that price point, and I didn't have a signed contract or a deposit. I had nothing. I've been in this situation several times before. Do I go ahead and book the flight? Do I trust that the client will come through? It felt similar to standing at the edge of that cliff, throwing my cash over the edge, hoping for profitable results from another unproven marketing strategy.

I checked online and found the event posted on BMC Software's website. All the details were there and it matched the information they had provided to me. The emails seemed legit and I took the plunge. It was already Saturday morning and my flight would leave on Tuesday afternoon. It was an insanely short lead time, but I felt good about it and started working on my presentation.

Credit Card Balance: $620 (January, 2014)

When I got on the plane, I still didn't have a signed contract or a deposit, but my business was going well and my credit cards had been almost entirely paid off. I was basically holding my breath and keeping my fingers crossed. I didn't even know at what hotel I would be staying! They just told me that someone would be at the airport waiting to pick me up when I got through customs. It was another adventure, Patrick style!

I arrived, got my bags, and walked out into the foyer where all the friends, relatives and drivers congregate, waiting for their passengers to arrive. There must have been at least two hundred people there and at least three- or four-dozen drivers holding signs with people's names on them. As you know, my name is a bit of a disaster, but that usually makes it fairly easy to see. Not this time. I didn't see it anywhere.

After walking back and forth a few times, I finally saw it. Whew! I missed it before because the driver was speaking with two other passengers who had also arrived, probably on the same flight as me. I introduced myself and immediately felt more comfortable. They were nice guys and they started telling me more about the event and the people who would be attending. It was far more information than I had received by email and based on their comments, I knew quickly that I would be making some adjustments to my PowerPoint slides.

We checked into the hotel and I met with all of my hosts. I met the guy from Singapore and his assistant, Milind, who worked out of an office in India. We all went to visit the room where the event would be taking place and quite casually, at the back of the room, Milind pulled out an envelope which was obviously full of cash. I was stunned. What's the right way to handle a situation like this?

Two decades earlier, I knew a few shady characters in Vancouver who were growing marijuana in their basement and selling it, wholesale, to the Hells Angels who took it across the US border and down to California. It was a well-established business in Vancouver, and the people who were involved knew exactly how things were supposed to work. I had no idea.

One time, I ended up in the car with a guy (let's call him Bill, just to keep it simple) who had to drop off some pot with his "associate" in the Hells Angels, a guy named Scotty. Bill had five pounds of pot, all dried and processed in half-pound bags, inside a yellow sports bag in the trunk. He drove to a parking lot where Scotty was waiting. Bill handed over the bag and Scotty handed over an envelope full of cash. They shook hands, turned around and walked back to their cars. I sat motionless in the passenger seat.

When Bill got back in the car, I asked, "Aren't you going to count the money?" Bill immediately told me to shut up and started driving away. When we were a safe distance away, he told me that you *never* count money with the Hells Angels! You take it, shake hands and walk away. "I mean, what else are you going to do?" he asked. "What if it's the wrong amount? What are you going to do about it?"

I learned some interesting lessons from that experience. It turns out that the criminal world actually has a lot more rules than the regular world. If you do something wrong, there are consequences and everyone knows it. Everyone knows who has more power and everyone knows who's doing whom a favor. When the Hells Angels are willing to buy your wholesale pot, they state the terms and you either agree or do not agree. If you agree, you do business. If you do not agree, you do not do business. But either way, you *never* count money in front of the Hells Angels. It's an insult. It's disrespectful. It makes you look like a chump.

So there I was in Dubai and Milind had just handed me an envelope full of cash. I remembered my experience with Bill immediately and simply said thank you, shook his hand and put the envelope in my suit pocket. "Aren't you going to count it?" he asked. "I'm sure it's fine, thank you," I replied and then went about my business as if nothing had happened. I could tell that he was shocked by my casual reaction, perhaps as shocked as I was years earlier with Bill. But it was pretty cool. I was James Bond.

I went upstairs and looked inside the envelope. It had 61 crisp one-hundred-dollar bills inside. It's amazing how happy you can feel when someone puts 61 crisp one-hundred-dollar bills in your hand. There's an urge to play with it and spread it across your bedspread, which is exactly what I did. I then lay down on top of the money and took selfies for at least five or ten minutes. I never posted those photos anywhere but have decided to post it in conjunction with this book. I look pretty happy!

http://www.keynotemastery.com/cash/

This happened on a smaller scale during my second trip to Dubai as well, the one with Tech Mahindra. They paid my 50% deposit before I left California but then paid the second half in cash in UAE Dirhams. It wasn't as much money, but it was still pretty cool. I remember exchanging it for US dollars at the airport, and the woman inside the booth looked at me funny when I handed her the wad. It was worth $1,500, and almost cleared her out of US dollars. Yes, I'm sure she had access to plenty more but for the moment, I was a high roller!

This is apparently quite common in the Middle East. When I went to Bahrain, my host, Ali Sakbar, told me that paying in cash was actually preferable. These things are fascinating. It varies by region. It's cultural. So now, when I'm speaking with a potential client in the Middle East and the negotiations are looking good, I usually mention that they're welcome to pay in cash if they like. It makes me look more savvy because it's probably unusual for an American to make that offer. And if they say yes, I'll probably end up taking more pictures!

57

THE SAVVY SPEAKER

I'm a big believer in looking savvy whenever possible, including both in person and also on your website. I think it dramatically increases your odds of getting booked. The word *savvy* refers to shrewdness and practical knowledge, especially in politics or business. Shrewdness sounds a bit ruthless to me, but practical knowledge is precisely what I'm referring to. Offering to accept payment in cash for Middle East events is savvy because it's common in real life, and there are plenty of other examples.

When people visit my website, I want them to see countless little details, either consciously or unconsciously, that make it look like I've done it all before. I want them to feel like they're dealing with a professional. I want to provide more structure and process than they expect. I have a saying that "leaders hate structure but followers love it," and it really applies in this case. When they contact me, I want them to immediately see structure around my business.

This applies to the information (like the frequently asked questions) included on my website, the forms, photos and biography available for them to use and my responses to their questions via email or on the phone. For example, when I'm quoting for an overseas event, I always mention that I request a three-night minimum when attending overseas events: two before my speaking session and one after. The reason is to ensure I don't arrive the night before a morning speaking session with an eight- or nine-hour time change and possibly a bunch of logistical and/or language hurdles to contend with. I want to make sure I can arrive, make my way to the hotel and get at least one good night's sleep before I need to speak.

The reality is that I don't always get three hotel nights for overseas events, but *asking* for them makes me look savvy. It makes it obvious that I've done this before and am taking precautions to ensure I do a good job. It makes them feel like they're dealing with a professional who is familiar with the risks involved.

Another example involves PowerPoint. When an event is booked and we're moving on to the planning process, I always tell the client that I'm using a 4:3 aspect ratio (as opposed to the wider 16:9 aspect ratio) for my PowerPoint slides. 99% of the time, they don't immediately know what that means, but I explain it in more detail and they then know what they need to check on. It relates to the screen dimensions and possibly their slide templates as well.

Again, I'm not married to my 4:3 aspect ratio. In many cases, I have transferred all my slides over to the 16:9 format. In fact, I believe the 16:9 will become the standard in the years ahead. The point is not to impose my preferences on their planning process. The point is to bring up a potential problem before they have thought about it themselves. They immediately understand that they're dealing with a professional.

I have a standard contract format. I have a PDF file with all of my wire transfer instructions spelled out. I have an updated W-9 form filled out and signed at the beginning of each year. I have a copy of my passport in PDF format for international events. All of these files are named according to a standard naming convention. I want everything I do to be structured and organized, resulting from many past experiences as a professional speaker.

Visit **Keynote**Mastery.com to download worksheet #15 on peripheral marketing tools.

Nobody wants to hire a newbie. Nobody wants to take a risk. They want to know that you've done this before and are ready for the obstacles and challenges you might encounter. By demonstrating that on your website and reinforcing with the business collateral you provide, you're reducing the risk for your clients. Take the time to develop this business collateral and incorporate as much of it onto your website as possible.

DISTRACTION-FREE PEOPLE

I've always wanted to surround myself with quality people, and I meet plenty on my travels. The people who attend conferences are generally those who can afford to go or those who achieved sufficient business success to earn them an invite. These were high performers. The people attending the Bloomberg dinners are the executives and sales dynamos of the cable affiliates. The financial advisors from Australia who attended the incentive trip in Bangkok were the top producers at Capstone. The Indian real estate developers who attended the conference in Moscow were those willing to invest in their businesses with educational content and networking opportunities.

Even *within* each event, I always meet the top people. If it's a corporate function, I usually meet the CEO and other top executives. If it's an association event, I meet the elected President and other board members, as well as the most prominent attendees. On a number of occasions, I met the mayors of local cities. In Bangkok and Moscow, I met the ambassadors of the visiting nationals. In Bogota, Colombia, I met a presidential candidate. Every time I'm on a trip, I'm introduced to a parade of successful and influential people.

As a speaker, you need to look the part. You have to dress for success, and anything that detracts from that image reduces the value you bring. I view these things as distractions. An extreme example might be a piece of toilet paper stuck to the bottom of your shoe. It's a distraction. But even if you're wearing a poorly tailored suit, it's a distraction. If you have a squeaky voice or a strong accent, it's a distraction. If you're significantly overweight or look unclean, those are distractions. As a speaker, you want to be distraction-free. You want to have nothing that distracts people from your content and your message.

This is also true for people in general. All of these high performers that I was meeting were, for the most part, distraction-free. They look fine. They speak fine. They dress fine. There's nothing immediately wrong with the picture. Everything is fine. And as simple as that sounds, it's actually quite uncommon. Most people have distractions of one kind or another. Some of them could be eliminated with a bit more attention to detail. Others are built in and can't be fixed. In either case, these distractions inevitably hold them back from further success in life.

Some people don't realize how important it is to simply be normal and appropriate in their respective work environments. I'm not suggesting we limit our unique qualities or back down from our convictions. I'm simply suggesting that we put some effort into looking and acting our best in work situations. It doesn't serve anyone to show up wearing dirty clothes and acting crazy. You're better off being distraction-free.

The frustrating thing is the differential between my work life and my personal life. When I'm traveling for work, I meet incredibly high-quality people but when I'm at home, it's rare for me to come across this same caliber. Many distraction-free people are salespeople or executives for large technology, financial or pharmaceutical companies. They work in tall office buildings in San Francisco or sprawling campuses in Silicon Valley. I'm self-employed and work from home. These are parallel worlds and rarely intersect.

Self-employed people, including me, are generally renegades or corporate misfits. They all felt compelled to go independent. In my case, I have always been fiercely independent and never did very well with supervision. If these kinds of people felt comfortable in corporate America, they'd probably stick with it. It's remarkably easy to make good money by working for someone else! Despite that, these people left the comfort of a regular paycheck and pursued their dreams on their own.

When I'm here at home, I do socialize with people. I do have friends but most of them are self-employed. I met many of them in my Entrepreneur & Small Business Academy. One time during one of our monthly meetings, I told the attendees that I was making progress but also struggling to pay my bills. Then, after admitting to my own financial reality, I asked how many of them were consistently profitable in their respective businesses. There were about 100 people in attendance and only 25 or 30 raised their hands.

The vast majority of self-employed professionals are struggling to pay their bills. It's true for real estate agents, insurance brokers, life coaches, financial planners and massage therapists. Most are barely making ends meet. The sad reality is that those who do succeed are less and less inclined to attend free networking events. Birds of a feather flock together. It's natural to seek out those who are achieving a similar level of success. Jim Rohn once said, "You become the average of the five people you spend the most time with." I'm always hoping to associate with people at my level or higher. When you're just getting started, every event qualifies. Since you're at the bottom, everyone is at your level or higher. But as you become more successful, fewer and fewer events fit the bill.

The result is that free networking events attract mostly struggling self-employed professionals. Like I said before, they're renegades and corporate misfits. The ones that are well put together soon become successful and then stop attending. That means the people who attend are almost never distraction-free, and it's precisely those distractions that hold them back from achieving success themselves.

This was the difference between my Meetup events and Edith Yeung's events. Mine were free and attracted people who were still struggling. Edith charged money for her events and attracted a much higher quality crowd as a result. And while Edith was charging $20 or $25 for most of her events, the events that hire professional speakers usually cost hundreds or thousands of dollars to attend and as such, attract an even higher caliber of people.

At the very top of the ladder, there are groups that cost tens of thousands of dollars to join, and a major benefit of membership is the knowledge that all the other members paid the same amount to participate. The cost immediately eliminates people who can't afford it, leaving only the affluent people behind. And I promise you that these people are usually sharp, attractive, intelligent and distraction-free people.

A friend of mine once bought a brand new Ferrari from the factory in Italy, just to be included in an exclusive Ferrari owners club. It cost him over $250,000 and the primary benefit was the opportunity to hang out with other wealthy Ferrari owners. There are similar clubs for antique gun collectors, yacht owners and angel investors. With the explosion of America's wealthy class, these groups are thriving and they're all full of distraction-free professionals.

I know that this discussion might be controversial to some but it's also a central tenet of our social order. It's always been this way. Look back to old aristocratic Europe and you find the same thing. The people at the top are generally attractive and well put together. They dress the part. They act the part. They fit in perfectly at the top. And if you want to make it to that social class, you need to start presenting yourself the same way.

Incidentally, I'm not suggesting that everyone needs to walk around in suits and ties or fancy dresses. The fashion trends today are far more casual and the tech-startup motif is characterized by jeans and t-shirts, but those who are distraction-free still stand out. Much of it boils down to the way you walk, the way you talk and the way you interact with others. Even visiting diplomats wear jeans and t-shirts sometimes!

If you want to be a professional speaker, work on eliminating distractions. If you want to be more successful in some other career, work on eliminating distractions. If you want to be a recognized authority in your field, work on eliminating distractions. If you do, you will start to stand out from the crowd and people will listen more to your comments and suggestions. They will listen more to your message, and that's ultimately where your value resides.

59

THE NATIONAL SPEAKERS ASSOCIATION (NSA)

The primary association for professional speakers is the National Speakers Association (NSA) and they have chapters across the country. Most chapters hold events each month and you can attend as a member or a non-member. Non-members pay a few dollars more. I've gone to a few of these meetings myself and even spoken at one once, but have never actually joined the association.

Believe it or not, one of the primary reasons that my participation has been sparse is that their events are held on Saturday mornings and it takes me about an hour to drive there from my place. I hate early mornings! I've also found that they devote a lot of time to the platform-speaking model. Nevertheless, I enjoyed the meetings I attended and would like to attend more in the future.

The NSA hosts annual conventions which are held in different cities each year. Although I've never attended one, I've wanted to for the past three years and couldn't because I was traveling in each case. The people who attend the national convention are established keynote speakers who are very serious about their businesses. I've heard that the sessions are powerful and the keynotes are awesome. I definitely plan to attend one in the near future.

You should also know that the NSA offers a Certified Speaking Professional (CSP) designation that is recognized in corporate circles. It's earned after being paid for a minimum of 250 presentations over a 10-year period and documenting a minimum of $50,000 in income from speaking fees during five of those 10 years. The certification has a variety of other requirements but the paid gigs are the most significant hurdles. Essentially, the CSP designation demonstrates that you are indeed an established professional speaker and that you have significant experience in the field.

At the time of this writing, I qualify easily for the CSP designation but have yet to do all the paperwork. Putting it all together would be a nightmare. I would also have to find ways of documenting my speaking fees for past events and, of course, become a member of the NSA as well. I'm not sure how important it is to have the CSP designation but it certainly can't hurt.

If you decide to become a keynote speaker yourself, I strongly recommend that you fill in the paperwork along the way. I'm not sure how I could document all my past speaking fees and it's precisely that challenge that has held me back from getting the process started in the first place. Once achieved, it represents another notch in your belt. It's more credibility. It's another brick in your fortress.

GOOGLE SLAP

Credit Card Balance: $0 (July, 2014)

T he long July 4th weekend in 2014 brought with it a cruel surprise. Over the years, my website had developed a respectable search engine ranking and I had done plenty to accentuate that. Google was delivering over 80% of my traffic and it was the lifeblood of my business. But on July 5th, the traffic dried up. At first, I thought it was just the long holiday weekend, but it continued for the next few days. My daily organic traffic dropped from 100+ per day to just three or four. My traffic was gone.

Google's search algorithm incorporates hundreds of factors for all websites to determine their rankings for any combination of keywords. These factors are essentially grouped into various sub-algorithms. For example, the Penguin algorithm deals with the Internet's link structure and evaluates websites based on the number of links pointing to them. Another algorithm is called Panda and it deals primarily with the quality of content on each website.

With search engine rankings in mind, I had tons of keyword-rich content written by ghostwriters in the Philippines and Pakistan, people I found on the oDesk.com (now UpWork.com) outsourcing website. It wasn't bad content, but it wasn't very high quality either. And although I will never have exact confirmation of what happened on July 5th of 2014, I believe the Panda 4.0 algorithm update wiped me off the map.

The extent of the damage was dramatic. As you probably know, my primary speaking-related website is my full name: PatrickSchwerdtfeger.com. Also, obviously, my last name is very long and quite unusual. Despite that, a Google search for "Patrick Schwerdtfeger" no longer delivered my own website! You had to scroll through four pages of other listings before my own site showed up. This was a death knell for me and I went into panic mode.

I follow a number of SEO experts, either on YouTube or through email newsletter subscriptions, and had considered hiring one to do a full site audit many times in the past. SEO has always been an important part of my business and I would undoubtedly benefit from any suggestions they might provide. So far, I had never pulled the trigger on a site audit but my current Google blackout (called a "Google slap" in SEO circles) changed that immediately.

I arranged for a $500 site audit and was put on a waiting list to have it completed. They told me it would take 10 to 15 days. I couldn't get it fast enough, but apparently there were plenty of other websites in the same situation and I had to wait my turn. My organic site traffic was near zero, and I was essentially watching my hard-fought career evaporate in front of my eyes.

Interestingly, after six days of almost zero organic traffic, my site suddenly popped back up with daily traffic similar to before, perhaps even a touch higher. I was still in the line-up for the site audit and decided not to change my order. The past six days had instilled the fear of God in me, and I was determined to do whatever I could to fortify my rankings on Google.

I read countless articles and blog posts about Panda during those six days, and it seemed that every time Google released an update to Penguin or Panda, they immediately followed the release with a second algorithm that analyzes the websites that were affected by the update. My website was obviously among those slapped by the Panda 4.0 release. They then go in and reinstate all the websites that were wrongly downgraded. I'm guessing this is what happened to me.

Some would tell me that I should've let it go at that point. Clearly, my site wasn't that bad after all and I should go along on my merry way, but that wasn't my reaction at all. My site was obviously pretty close to the line between "white hat" and "black hat," and I needed to make adjustments as a result. About a week after being reinstated, I got my 63-page site audit from the SEO guy. Wow! 63 pages? I had a lot of work to do!

The recommendations weren't actually that bad but there were certainly some areas I needed to address. First, my site was only moderately mobile friendly and second, it wasn't "responsive design." These two labels are related to each other. *Mobile friendly* refers to the site's performance on mobile devices and *responsive design* means it presents the information differently depending on the size of screen. If you're visiting the site from a small mobile screen, the site looks different than it would on a full-sized laptop or desktop screen.

I decided to completely redesign my site on a new and fully responsive theme. It was a huge job and the upcoming Labor Day weekend was the perfect time to get started. Most people would redo the website on a separate private server, get everything just right and then switch the old site to the new one by flipping a switch. The problem with this approach is that (1) I had no idea how to build a site on a private server and (2) it would eliminate the incentive to finish quickly. I decided to do the redesign live.

As you've undoubtedly figured out by now, I did the redesign myself. I've never been much of a web designer, but do know a few things about the WordPress platform and didn't want someone else to come in and build something that I couldn't easily understand myself afterwards. I had hired someone to build the site for my third book, *Marketing Shortcuts for the Self-Employed* and always regretted that decision, because I was basically afraid of changing anything after the initial build.

WordPress (and dozens of other website-building platforms) are getting better and better all the time. I strongly encourage you to learn these platforms for yourself. It's not that hard and you'll be infinitely more empowered when you know exactly how your website was built. You'll be able to update it and make improvements and adjustments any time you like and will probably be amazed at how quickly you get comfortable with the process.

When I first met Josh in 2006, he was already experimenting with Content Management Systems (CMS) like WordPress, Joomla and Drupal. I had no experience building websites before, but he convinced me to give these CMS platforms a try. I hated it at first but learned quickly. Meanwhile, the software was improving at the same time, making these platforms easier and easier to use. Today, WordPress is an extremely powerful and flexible platform and I would recommend it to anyone.

With my redesign approaching quickly, I looked at my analytics for the past year and sorted all of my pages according to the traffic they had received, respectively. At 2:00 PM on Friday afternoon, I uploaded the new theme and immediately started recoding individual pages, starting with my homepage, contact page, programs page and "Strategic Business Insights" video blog page.

It was a marathon. I sat in front of my computer for at least 16 hours each day, redoing each page and then making adjustments to ensure it looked the way I wanted it to look. Any time you try to use new technology for the first time, there are millions of problems and hiccups along the way, and this was no different. But by

Monday evening, I had completely redesigned my top 16 pages, which accounted for about 70% of my traffic.

I spent every day that following week digging down into smaller and smaller pages. Each one presented its own challenges but they got done, one by one, and I learned a *ton* about my new theme and the various features it offered its users. By the end of the week, I had updated the vast majority of my site, accounting for over 91% of my traffic, and could start getting back to my other responsibilities again.

Now, the cold, hard truth. I'm thrilled with my new site. I think it looks much better and it caters directly to Google's stated preference for mobile-friendly websites, but the conversion rate has dropped. Ever since the redesign, my conversions have dropped off. My traffic is the same, even a bit higher, but my bookings are down. It's surprising because my new site looks so much more professional than the old one—but the numbers speak for themselves. My business is down.

Some people have told me to revert back to the old site, but I can't do that. The Google slap scared me too much. It's more important to have organic traffic to my site than to have that traffic convert into business. If the traffic goes away, I will lose my ability to make conversions at all. At least this way, I am still getting decent traffic and I can work on improving conversions over time.

I've had many conversations about the drop and I do have a theory about it, but you might think I'm nuts. Then again, you probably think that already. I actually think my new site looks a bit too good. I think it makes me look too expensive.

There are many different types of buyers when it comes to professional speakers and those searching on Google probably have a budget of between $3,000 and $6,000 on average. They don't *all* fall into that bracket but many of them do, and they might see my new website and assume that I'm more expensive. Of course, I have no idea if this is true or not, but it remains my best theory of what happened.

The question then becomes: what should I do about it? I've tried to include new verbiage about my fees being negotiable and the many factors that impact speaking fees, but it hasn't made a huge difference so far. I've also added larger call-to-action buttons but am still not back to the run rate that I had before. I've even thought about referencing lower fees on the site directly but that would eliminate my highest-paying opportunities.

I don't know the answer. Online, you can measure everything but inevitably, you never know exactly what your website visitors are thinking. I will continue to make adjustments and, hopefully, improve my conversion statistics incrementally. But at the same time, it's forced me to think about other marketing channels that are more in my own control. I will tell you about a few of those ideas before the end of the book. I'm actually pretty excited about the possibilities.

BOOK MARKETING

Book marketing sucks. It's difficult and by the time you read this, I'll be deep in the process again. I've gone through this three times before and have thought long and hard about the marketing plan I'd like to execute this fourth time around. But until I pull the trigger, I honestly have no idea which elements will be successful and which will not. It's a gamble and costs a lot of money. I'd like to explain the process because you may end up going through it yourself.

Let me be on the record: I strongly recommend writing nonfiction books for your own business. Even if you have no interest in becoming a keynote speaker, becoming an *author* will undoubtedly improve your positioning as an expert in your field. If you're a consultant, a trainer, a self-employed service professional (like a real estate agent, insurance broker, mortgage banker, financial planner, chiropractor, physical therapist, life coach, bookkeeper, contractor, attorney, etc.), I highly recommend writing nonfiction books on your subject.

Also, there's magic to your first book. You only become an author once. You could go on to write 100 books, but you only become an author once and from that day forward, you can position yourself differently. You're an author and people respect that. Most people dream about writing a book but few ever do. Once

248

you've crossed that milestone, they'll treat you differently. They'll treat you with more respect.

Most people think that writing the book is the hard part. Nope. That's the easy part. The hard part is *marketing* the book. If you self-publish, the marketing is 100% your responsibility. Contrary to popular belief, that is essentially true for traditional publishers as well. Most people believe *they* take care of the marketing for you. Nope. They will only accept your proposal if they believe you have a sufficient "platform" to promote the book yourself. Once the book has been released, they will roughly match your own marketing efforts. If you do nothing, they will also do nothing.

Your platform refers to your following. How many people are following your work? How big is your email list? How many followers do you have on Twitter or Facebook? Do you have influence within a large community? Do you have influential contacts who will publicly endorse your book to their own audiences? And beyond all that, what resources are you willing to commit to the marketing process? Where will you spend your marketing dollars? And what is your overall marketing budget?

There are many ways to build a platform. You can start blogging and develop a following that way. You can start a video blog like me and accumulate subscribers over time. You can start a podcast on iTunes or an online community on Facebook or LinkedIn. They're all great options, but there's really no guarantee that your audience will grow. There are plenty of people who are trying to grow their following and most never get much traction.

Perhaps the people involved give up too quickly. Perhaps they don't have the discipline to produce new content on a regular basis, or perhaps the content they produce isn't compelling enough to keep people coming back for more. The sad reality is that some of us are natural leaders and others are not. Some of us are more funny and clever than others. Some of us are more fun to hang out with than others. All of these factors impact our ability to succeed.

In my case, my "Beyond the Rate" podcast did quite well, but there were few to pick from back then. I've never had much success blogging and while my video blog continues to grow, the numbers aren't accelerating. It's linear growth. Yes, over time, the numbers add up, but I can't boast the exponential growth that other content producers sometimes achieve. I certainly haven't become a YouTube celebrity!

The net result is that I need a pay-to-play option. I need to utilize paid mediums that will get my work in front of the right eyeballs. Options include promoted posts on Facebook, sponsored tweets on Twitter, promoted videos on YouTube, targeted keywords on Google, banner advertising on relevant websites and paid placement in monthly newsletters—and there's nothing wrong with any of these paid options.

Most of the famous information marketers that we have come to know originally got our attention with paid advertising. Once we engage with an offer, we're added to their list and promptly forget that the connection started with an advertisement. We become familiar with their work and assume that they achieved their success through exclusively organic channels. Not so. People like Brendon Burchard, Tony Robbins, Robert Kiyosaki, Deepak Chopra, Wayne Dyer and Brian Tracy have all used paid advertising extensively to build their followings and grow their businesses.

People have no idea how many areas of our world are actually pay-to-play. When you see people being interviewed on the major television networks, most of those people paid to be there. Yes, these programs have their favorite contributors who are invited back and, of course, there are true subject-matter experts that are brought in when circumstances require that type of analysis, but the other contributors have usually paid for that placement.

There are public relations (PR) firms that specialize in this sort of thing. Annie Jennings in New York is known for her pay-per-performance model. When you hire Annie Jennings, she will guarantee that you end up on regional or national programs, be they radio or television, and you pay ahead of time for the placements you want to get. Everything has a price. Everything.

Most airports in the United States have a Hudson Bookstore (or one of their competitors) in the terminal. Those are pay-to-play models as well. Every book in those stores is a paid placement. Shelf space at eye level costs about $10,000 per month, being on the featured table in the center of the store costs about $30,000 per month and shelf-space on the concourse-facing island at the front of the store costs between $50,000 and $70,000 per month.

Keep in mind that Hudson Bookstores get the standard retail markup on your books as well. You sell it to them at wholesale and they sell it at retail, so they get that markup *plus* the monthly placement fee. They have about 300 stores across the country. These paid placement contracts are rarely profitable on their own but if you (the author) have a big "backend" to offer, it can be a very savvy and highly targeted book-marketing strategy.

In this context, a *backend* refers to the consulting, training and speaking services that you offer to corporate clients who need your expertise. The last time I was in an airport, the two books on the front island were *Good to Great* by Jim Collins and *The 10x Rule* by Grant Cardone, and they both have huge backend programs. They both charge celebrity speaking fees and offer expensive training and consulting services. So for them, it's a great strategy.

People who are not in business often think airports are full of vacationers, but that's not true at all. Airports are full of business travelers. They might be trainers, salespeople, senior managers, executives, consultants or speakers like me. It's a very specific demographic. These people are decision makers with medium-to-large corporations and they all have budgets to play with. If you're selling consulting, training or speaking, Hudson Bookstores are perfect.

It's also interesting to note that most people never read another book after they graduate from high school or college. Meanwhile, CEOs and other business leaders often read 50 or 60 books each year. These leaders are frequently *looking* for new titles because they go through books so quickly. Leaders are readers; it's true. And if you want to become a better leader yourself, the very best thing you can do is to read more.

The point is that you're automatically putting your expertise in front of business leaders by writing nonfiction books. You bypass the average people because they don't read. But leaders *are* readers and if you have a good book in a business category, you're directly in the line of fire for decision makers who need your services. In football, they talk about putting yourself "in a position to win." By writing nonfiction books, you're putting yourself in a position to win.

The last thing we need to cover is that your book is little more than a fancy business card. Few authors earn significant profits by selling books. Some do but they're the exceptions. Most nonfiction authors earn money by selling backend services, with their book acting as the initial introduction and nothing more. Jim Collins and Grant Cardone both have great business books, and they both offer extensive business services to corporations. The Hudson Bookstores represent the perfect targeting for them.

All of these things apply to my books as well, including this one. I'm not expecting to make much money on the book itself. In fact, the money I plan to spend on the marketing plan will undoubtedly eat up the profits and probably much more. My backend is keynote speaking and I also have a number of resources for aspiring speakers. I'll tell you about those shortly. And yes, I am considering the Hudson Bookstores myself.

If you're an author or plan to become one, you need to put some serious thought into your marketing plan. There are countless different strategies you can use, and the most effective strategies shift as the years go by. There's always some new medium that didn't exist a few years ago. The point is that I recommend that you promote your book as heavily as you possibly can. It's worth it.

The average book sells fewer than 250 copies per year and fewer than 3,000 books over its lifetime. Very few books sell more than 5,000 copies and far fewer sell more than 15,000 copies. Meanwhile, the books that *do* sell that many copies start to benefit from the higher awareness and actually take on a momentum of their own. The hardest part is to get past 5,000 copies and then up to 15,000 copies. But beyond that point, there has already been enough traction that the book will start to have familiarity in relevant circles.

Visit **Keynote**Mastery.com to download worksheet #16 on book-marketing options.

Currently, one of the most important ingredients is Amazon reviews. Amazon sells the vast majority of books these days, and the books with more than 100 or 200 reviews sell much better than those with fewer reviews. It's also important to know that Amazon now filters reviews and deletes reviews that appear unnatural or possibly paid for. Never pay for book reviews. There are lots of pay-to-play marketing options that I support but paid book reviews are *not* among them.

The #1 nicest thing you could do for me is write a review for this book on Amazon and tell your friends about it!

If you've gotten to this part of the book, thank you! Seriously, I am quite grateful. You're in the home stretch and I truly hope you have found value in my story. I've tried to be completely transparent and honest with my journey including the good, the bad and the ugly. I want this book to change people's lives. I want them to see what's possible with slow steady progress. I want them to see the innately human journey that it was for me and, hopefully, take some solace in the challenges you inevitably encounter. But if this book is going to be a success, I need your help.

Please take a few minutes and write a review. Give it as many stars as you think it deserves. I'm not asking for charity. I'm asking for an honest review that benefits future readers. People on Amazon make their purchase decisions based on (1) the title and description of the book, (2) the number of reviews it has and (3) the contents of those reviews. Please be honest and share your thoughts—good, bad or indifferent—for others to see.

As a token of my appreciation, I am giving away my $49 *How to Become a TEDx Speaker* ebook to everyone who writes a review on Amazon. Yes, it's that important. So regardless how many stars you give the book and regardless of the comments or critiques you include, please send an email to reviews@keynotemastery.com and include a screen capture of your review on Amazon and we will reply with a direct link to the download page.

Also, if you found value in the book, please tell your friends about it. Whom do you know that's self-employed? Whom do you know who's trying to build credibility in their career? Whom do you know who wants to become a recognized expert in their field? And, of course, whom do you know who wants to become a keynote speaker? Word-of-mouth is the only reason any book ever achieves sustained success.

It's easy to spend money to get your book on the bestsellers' list. If you have enough money, it can be virtually guaranteed. But if the book doesn't deliver real value, the sales dry up as soon as the marketing stops. Keep this in mind if you plan to write books yourself. Focus on delivering value and don't be shy about appealing to your readers directly. That's precisely what I'm doing here!

62

THE KEYNOTE MASTERY PROGRAM

In early 2012, with my revenue down 40% from the previous year, I decided to create and sell a live program devoted entirely to the profession of keynote speaking. I've always had lots of people ask me about my career, and if you decide to become a keynote speaker yourself, you'll probably experience the same thing. It's a sexy career. Most people are fascinated when they hear what I do. They want to hear more, and many of them want to learn how to do it themselves. Even established platform speakers are often eager to learn.

I held a free event at a church in Berkeley and promoted it to my Entrepreneur & Small Business Academy. About 250 people showed up. I told them about my career path, much as I have done here in this book. I told a few stories and gave them a glimpse into this career path. They loved it and it was really fun for me too. I was proud of what I had accomplished. At the end of my presentation, I told them about my brand new Keynote Mastery program. It was a live two-day training and I delivered it for the first time in March of that year.

It's important to note that most programs about speaking are actually about platform speaking, not keynote speaking. Brendon Burchard, James Malinchak and Steve Harrison all have programs about becoming a speaker, but they focus on promoting your own events and selling products or programs at the back of the room. These are great programs, by the way, but they're not teaching keynote. They're teaching platform. I've never found a program that's devoted entirely to keynote speaking.

My inaugural Keynote Mastery program went well and I was asked to deliver it again in a virtual format in August of that year. Based on my experience with the first edition, I made dozens of improvements and adjustments and delivered it on five conference calls the second time around. After that program was over, I sold the recordings and worksheets on my website for other aspiring speakers. It was never a significant part of my business but it did a great job of answering common questions about this career.

With the release of this book, I'm officially launching the newly updated Keynote Mastery program. If you enjoyed my approach to this book, you'll love the program. It's the full-meal deal. I disclose everything. Although the program covers all aspects of the business, the most important section is the one about marketing. I've broken down all of the proven marketing strategies that I've used to build my own career and organized them by circuit.

1. Free Circuit
2. Cheap Circuit
3. Pro Circuit
4. Celebrity Circuit

Yes, there are indeed marketing strategies that will get you into the celebrity circuit. They cost money and definitely require a leap of faith, but it can be done. That's what this program is all about: getting it *done*. Bottom line: if I knew everything I know now back in 2007, I could've made the same progress in half the time. With the Keynote Mastery program, starting from scratch, you can become a full-time keynote speaker within two or three years. It's the best career in the world, and it can be built from the ground up. Learn more at KeynoteMastery.com.

The Keynote Mastery community is an even more valuable resource. I'll be hosting an educational webinar at the beginning of each month and will also host a live conference call to answer questions at the end of each month. Members will have access to all previous sessions. In addition, the community will feature a private forum for members where we can all share ideas, successes and failures with each other. Forums are extremely powerful tools when they're used by focused people who are serious about their careers. The community will also include private Facebook and LinkedIn groups.

These are the resources I wish I had along my own journey. They didn't exist back then. Actually, they *still* don't, at least not with such a specific focus on keynote speaking. I'd like to continue my career as part of a community. I'd like to meet my fellow keynote speakers and be part of a *tribe* rather than constantly struggling as a lone ranger and guessing at the right path forward. I have never found a mentor over the years, mainly because true keynote speakers don't travel in packs. They tend to fly solo and it's almost impossible to learn how they're marketing their businesses. The Keynote Mastery Community will change that.

THE SPEAKER SYNDICATE

The last thing I'd like to tell you about is the business that I'm most excited about. As you already know, the organic path to building a big following is difficult. It doesn't work for all people. And while my own efforts have thankfully been enough to keep me moving forward, they never created the momentum I was hoping for. I need a pay-to-play model. I want to do aggressive outbound marketing, both online and offline.

The problem is that it always costs a ton of money and the results are never guaranteed. I always feel like I'm standing on the edge of that cliff, throwing money over the edge. On the other hand, there are a few strategies that are virtually guaranteed to deliver results but they're impractical to pursue by individual speakers. They cost too much and take too much time. Let me give you one example.

There are well over 30,000 professional meeting planners in the United States. These are the people who hire keynote speakers for corporate events. I'd like to send postcards to each one of them, six times each year. They say that postcard campaigns rarely deliver a good return on investment (ROI) until the recipients have received at least seven postcards over time. Once they've received your marketing at least seven times, they start to recognize you and the ROI improves.

This strategy is most common in the real estate industry. They call it "farming," and I've met many agents who have farmed certain neighborhoods and communities for years and even decades. After a while, everyone in the community becomes familiar with you and when they're ready to buy or sell a house, they think of you first. Farming works. In fact, as the amount of junk mail has gone down in recent years (replaced, mostly, by online advertising), the ROI of direct mail has actually gone up.

As an individual speaker, I would never be able to afford a postcard campaign like that. If it costs 40¢ per postcard, it would cost $12,000 for each mailing or $72,000 for six mailings in one year. That's a lot of money! It wouldn't be practical anyway. Over time, it would generate more opportunities than I could fill on my own, so I'd have to select some subset of the total list to balance the marketing expense with the potential payoff. Even with only a subset to focus on, I would have to wait over a year to evaluate the ROI properly.

Meeting Professionals International (MPI) is an association of meeting planners, but it's not the only one. There's also the Professional Convention Management Association (PCMA) and the Society of Incentive Travel Executives (SITE) and the Financial and Insurance Conference Planners (FICP) and many more. I'd love to have banner ads on their websites and possibly program inserts at their annual conventions. There are so many different ways to target corporate meeting and event planners, both online and offline, but there's no practical way to do it all and optimize the campaigns.

This is why you rarely see advertisements for speakers. If you go online and search for "keynote speaker" or "motivational speaker," you'll see several pay-per-click ads from various speakers and speakers' bureaus, but their footprint is small. Nobody has a business model big enough to support a large immersive marketing campaign. But what if there was a way that individual speakers could pool their marketing resources and fund an optimized co-op advertising campaign as a group?

With this book, I'm thrilled to launch the Speaker Syndicate. It's a pay-to-play model where individual speakers can pool resources and pursue an aggressive and endlessly calibrated marketing strategy as a group … and I'll be the very first customer! The SpeakerSyndicate.com website is a directory of participating speakers with the most robust search-and-sort capability available in the industry. Meeting planners can search for speakers and sort the results based on a wide variety of different variables.

There are varying buy-in levels for participating speakers. Users of the site will not be able to see which speakers paid more and which paid less, but the results of their searches will be sorted according to those participation levels. The money will go towards the various advertising channels, and every participant will get detailed information on the monthly spend as well as the results and analytics on the website.

The hardest part of becoming a keynote speaker is getting your content in front of the right eyeballs. That's been my struggle from the start. If I could get my website and video blog in front of more relevant eyeballs, my business would increase. It's that simple. Believe me, I monitor my conversion rate feverishly and have a very clear idea of how many website views it takes for me to secure one speaking engagement. If I had more views, I would secure more business.

The Speaker Syndicate is designed to solve that problem—not just for me but for other aspiring speakers too. If we had 100 participating speakers who were contributing an average of $1,500 per month, we would have $150,000 per month to spend on the program. Do you know what we could do with that type of marketing budget? It would generate an absolutely *massive* footprint in the meeting-planner community, and we would all have more relevant eyeballs than we could handle!

This point is worth repeating. Once established, the Speaker Syndicate will have the largest footprint in the industry. Meeting planners will not be able to turn around without seeing our brand. Every meeting planner in the country will know the Syndicate, and the speakers on the list will share the resulting exposure for their mutual benefit. It'll be an exclusive club of high-visibility speakers.

Add your name to the waiting list at SpeakerSyndicate.com

The biggest challenge for the Syndicate will be quality control. We'll need to ensure that all of our speakers are established professionals who have respectable websites and professional demo videos. A minimum monthly buy-in requirement will immediately weed out those who aren't serious about the business, but I'm sure there will still be many applications from speakers who haven't yet refined their topics and programs. Participation will be limited to those who are ready for the big leagues.

Speakers in the Syndicate will have a minimum speaking fee of $5,000, further helping to ensure an established group. Of course, speakers will have the flexibility to negotiate discounts with clients but the listed fees will start at $5,000. It will be very important to guarantee a professional caliber from all of our speakers. The application process will be stringent and include professional qualification requirements.

We also have to deliver value for the meeting planners. For example, I'm tempted to offer a 100% money-back guarantee for any speaker we represent. If such a refund is ever requested, the Syndicate will pay it and remove the speaker from the platform. Depending on the circumstances, the speaker might be given an opportunity to pay the refund directly and then remain in the community, but such an opportunity would only be granted once.

This type of guarantee will obviously cost money and other things will too. The site will constantly be updated and improved, ensuring the most efficient and effective search and sort functions for users. We will also have experienced marketing professionals on staff, tasked with campaign optimization and split A/B testing to identify the most effective strategies, ad text, imagery, retargeting opportunities, calls-to-action and postcard designs, among other things. A percentage of the revenue will be allocated to these administration functions. Over time, we will all share in the largest and most optimized marketing funnel in the industry.

The point is that the Speaker Syndicate is a way for me and other professional speakers to take our businesses out of the sandbox and onto the freeway. It's the Edith Yeung approach to professional speaking. Just like her San Francisco Entrepreneur Meetup and her BizTechDay conference, this is a real business model supported by a real marketing budget. For the speakers who want to explode their exposure and drive their businesses to the next level, the Speaker Syndicate is a dream come true.

Visit SpeakerSyndicate.com for more details.

I'm very excited about this project and can't wait to see who else wants to join the team. We will not begin promoting the platform until we have a good selection of speakers involved. We need to have enough speakers to offer a good variety for meeting planners. But once we hit that initial threshold, we'll launch the site with a bang and start calibrating strategies immediately. Over time, we will identify the most effective marketing channels and maximize the return on investment (ROI) for our member speakers.

UNEXPECTED BLESSINGS

I t's been six years since my dad passed away and we're still visiting my mom every three months. The seniors facility that she lives in has about 200 residents. My mother has more individual care than anyone else in the building. We still have some of the same caregivers that we started with in 2007 and they spend 12 hours each day with her. The other residents call her Queen Elizabeth (her name is Elizabeth). The caregivers keep her clean, help her eat her meals and take her for walks every day.

She doesn't speak anymore and is only somewhat aware of her surroundings. She has no idea if she's in Vancouver or Switzerland or somewhere else, but none of that matters. She has excellent care, a daily routine and lots of companionship. Our visits actually make things more difficult because they're a departure from her daily routine. She's always happy on the first day of our visits but then gets agitated and confused on day two, three and four. Nevertheless, those visits have been therapeutic for me.

My mother's judgments are gone now. I sit beside her and show her photos or tell her stories. During my last visit, I read her about 140 pages of this manuscript, omitting the parts about her or my dad. She likes to hold hands and even smiles from time to time. It's sweet. It's given me a chance to let go of the anger I had earlier in life. The last six years have been an exercise in forgiveness. It's impossible to be angry at someone in her situation, regardless of the bad memories or hurt feelings from years gone by.

These are gifts. My father's Parkinson's medication made him more emotional. Although he hated that, it allowed me to feel more connected with him before he passed away. My mother was diagnosed with a mental illness. That diagnosis helped me release her judgments from my teenage years. And now, her illness has stripped those judgments away and allowed me to see her sweetness once again. The horrible circumstances they both struggled with were unexpected blessings in my life.

When my dad died, I cut the hospital wristband from his arm. I still have it today. One day, my mother will join him in the afterlife and I will put that wristband in her coffin. Despite all the chaos and madness, they were 100% devoted to each other. They loved each other. They always wanted to be together and I will be happy when they can be together again.

65

THE SURPRISING TRUTH

S o here I sit, writing this book. I'm 44 years old and I've been a full-time speaker since 2007, when I was 36. Looking back now, I wish I would've gotten started earlier. I always believed that I needed an indisputable victory in some other field in order to become a professional speaker. I thought I needed to be a gold medalist at the Olympics or the quarterback of the Dallas Cowboys. I thought I needed to land a plane on the Hudson River like Captain "Sully" Sullenberger or cut my own arm off like Aron Ralston, but it's not true. I didn't need any of those things. I just needed to embrace this career and start building it, brick by brick, over time.

The truth is that the process *became* the credential. The journey *became* the destination. My indisputable victory is that I never had an indisputable victory ... and I succeeded anyway! I never gave up. My determination and tenacity brought me to hundreds of different events in dozens of cities around the world, and that experience gave me the credibility I lacked at the beginning. That's my surprising truth. That's what's remarkable. That's what people are most fascinated by.

Most people believe the secret to success is timing. It's not. The secret to success is *time*. It's staying in one field long enough to secure your place in the market. Three different things happen when you stay in one field for a long time. First, you end up becoming incredibly proficient at the skills required. Second, everyone in your extended network understands what you do and they're increasingly likely to refer you and possibly hire you themselves. And third, you become part of a smaller and smaller group who have been doing it as long as you. You become a veteran in the field.

Don't underestimate the significance of this. Becoming very good at your work, for example, is the central pillar of long-term success. When you're the best at what you do, you don't have to do any marketing at all. People spread the word for you, even if you don't want them to. As a speaker, I always know when I truly knocked it out of the park because I get more spinoff business as a result. And if I'm not getting those referrals, I know that I need to refine my programs further.

The familiarity in your extended network is also critical. When you've been in one field for a long time, your network becomes increasingly familiar with your value proposition. On top of that, your network grows over time as you work with more and more clients. That means you're increasingly likely to get referrals as the years go by. Every time you speak, you're in front of 100, 200 or 300+ people. All of those people gain some peripheral knowledge of you and your programs. Once you've been doing this for a while, that increasing familiarity starts to pay dividends.

The third point is, of course, related to the first two, but it also has its own dynamic. A friend of mine has been a professional speaker for 35 years. 35 years! Over that amount of time, he has literally spoken for every type of business and traveled to every corner of the globe. His experience is so thorough that new people who find him for the first time are blown away, and his conversion rate is much higher as a result.

At this stage, I've been speaking for eight years and next year, it will be nine. The hardest day is your first. After that, each successive day you start accumulating more experience. You're accumulating bricks, one by one, and stacking them on top of each other.

At first, it doesn't look like much. But over time, it starts to take shape and become more and more impressive. Like I've said before, success is the accumulation of 10,000 tiny victories and 100,000 tiny failures!

If you have a dream you've been waiting to pursue, wait no longer. I'm not suggesting you need to quit your job and risk all of the stability you've worked hard for, but I *am* suggesting you start taking action today. Les Brown says, "You don't have to be great to get started, but you have to get started to be great." I suppose reading this book is one tiny step in that process. I've read dozens of books that have inspired me to move my business forward and I hope this book has played that role for you.

As you now know all too well, my life is far from perfect. I'm stubborn and don't give up easily. It's forced me to live a lonely life so far, and that's mostly my own fault. I accept that, but I'm also trying really hard to bring balance back into my life. I believe the victory in my career will help me find the other pieces that have eluded me so far. Everything in life is connected. When something is going badly in your life, it bleeds over into other areas, but when something is going really well, that bleeds over as well.

In the end, I achieved my dream. My dream came true. There were so many people along the way who told me that I was crazy, or at least alluded as much, but my persistence paid off. I *knew* this was possible. I *knew* that I would win eventually. The only way to lose is to quit. As long as you keep stacking those bricks, your inevitable success gets closer every day. There was never one defining event that secured my success. But over time, I did indeed turn the corner. I got my day in the sun.

Now, it's your turn. I have two challenges for you. First, pursue your dreams! Whether you want to become a keynote speaker or build your reputation in some other area, start stacking those bricks. You don't need anything more than what you have already. Nobody is born an expert. Everybody starts at zero. It's a building process for everyone, but some start building a lot earlier than others, and some just build faster. Don't wait any longer. There's a dream out there waiting to become your reality!

Second, tell your story openly and honestly. Life is more fulfilling when you're willing to be vulnerable with those you're close to. Brené Brown calls it "whole-hearted" living. I call it being real and being human. It's living in the deep end of the pool and it's the birthplace of empathy and compassion. Life is pretty awesome sometimes but the victories are twice as sweet when they're contrasted against the struggles. We all experience them both, victories and struggles, and I encourage you to share them with others.

The road to *being* is through *doing*! Please put the lessons in this book into practice in your own career. I would love to hear from you if you have comments about the book or are interested in the Keynote Mastery Community or the Speaker Syndicate. It's time to come down onto your goals from above! It's time to think bigger! I truly hope that my story has left you with hope and direction. It's been a pleasure to share it with you, and I hope that we can continue this connection in the future.